Great Little Quilts

Great Little Quilts

45 Antique Crib and Doll-size Quilts
with Patterns and Directions

By Eleanor Levie
Photography by André Gillardin

Harry N. Abrams, Inc., Publishers, New York

To Ruth Levie and Eleanor Harrington,
who have always set a great example for me

Editor: Ellen Rosefsky
Designer: Darilyn Lowe

Library of Congress Cataloging-in-Publication Data

Levie, Eleanor.
   Great little quilts: 45 antique crib and doll-size quilts with patterns
and directions/by Eleanor Levie; photography by André Gillardin.
        p. cm.
   Includes bibliographical references.
   ISBN 0–8109–3353–5
   1. Quilting—Patterns.   2. Doll quilts.   3. Crib quilts.
   I. Title.
   TT835.L47   1990
   746.9′7—dc20   90–30559
                                                                      CIP

Published in 1990 by Harry N. Abrams, Incorporated, New York
A Times Mirror Company

Printed and bound in Hong Kong

Contents

Introduction 8

Chapter 1: Basics 11

    Amish One-Patch 13
    Checkerboard 14
    Postage Stamp 16
    Nine-Patch Doll Quilt 17
    Nine-Patch Crib Quilt 20
    Amish Irish Chain 21
    Jacob's Ladder 24

Chapter 2: Rhythms 27

    Birds in the Air 29
    Pandora's Box 32
    Honeybee 33
    Strawberries 38
    Rising Sun 42

Chapter 3: Whimsy 45

    Ships 48
    Bowtie 50
    Pinwheel 51
    Sunbonnet Ladies 53
    Overall Sam 58
    Donkey 62
    Elephant 63

Chapter 4: Sentiment 65

    Diamonds 67
    Posies Round the Square 68
    Rose of Sharon 71
    Whitework 76
    Single Wedding Ring 78
    Wreath 80
    Iris 82

Chapter 5: Multiples 85

Fleur-de-Lis   87
Basket   89
Hourglass   90
Oak Leaf and Double X   94
Hand-Stitched Broken Dishes   98
Machine-Stitched Broken Dishes   99
Framed Medallion   101

Chapter 6: Graphics 105

Amish Shadows   107
Log Cabin   109
Carpenter's Square   110
Sawtooth and Cloverleaf   114
Sawtooth   117
Streak o'Lightning   118
Village Church   122

Chapter 7: Dimension 125

Bull's-Eye Square   127
Basketweave   128
Contained Crazy Quilt   130
Yo-Yo   133
Pleated Log Cabin   134

General Directions 137

Acknowledgments 140

Dealers 142

Bibliography 143

Single Wedding Ring. c. 1930. 27⅜" x 35½".
Collection of the author, courtesy of Yankee
Doodle Dandy

Introduction

I have always loved antique and contemporary textiles, particularly quilts. My experience as a needlework and crafts editor for several leading women's magazines has given me an opportunity to study how classic and untraditional quilts are constructed, which has increased my admiration for them. I enjoy browsing in antique quilt shops and going to antiques shows, where I head straight for the quilts. Most of the quilts in this book are borrowed from dealers, though some come from private collections, including my own.

I collect and buy what I love, and invariably my choice is a small piece. I don't think anybody ever outgrows a fascination for miniatures. For me, that encompasses dolls, dollhouses, and most of all, intimately scaled textiles of all types. While I plan to enjoy the small antique quilts I have bought for the rest of my life, I rationalize their expense knowing that they are often even better investments than full-size antique quilts. There are several reasons for this: First, crib and doll-size quilts are more rare than full-size quilts, since anything used by children is susceptible to extreme wear and tear. In most cases small antique quilts have not survived. Second, in earlier centuries, infant mortality was high, and small quilts were often buried with the baby. Those, of course, are completely lost to us. Third, at a time when quilts are appreciated as art, or at least as high forms of folk art, any quilt is going to be of a higher value if it is an original and visually arresting piece. In a small piece, a quiltmaker has less at stake in terms of time and effort. She can afford to be more daring and unique in her design. Fourth, small quilts are coveted because they are easy to display and do not require a huge amount of wall space.

Because antique crib and doll-size quilts are relatively rare, we need to conserve them. Natural and artificial light, humidity and excessive handling, and undue stress from certain mounting devices can damage a quilt. The best protection is to wrap an old quilt in acid-free tissue paper, put it in a dark, dry closet, and never open the door. But if you want to enjoy your quilt as I do, such measures may seem extreme. As the Chinese have tended their beautiful silk textiles for centuries, rotating a collection makes sense, making sure that a quilt does not remain in the same spot for more than three to six months at a time. In any case, we should treat our collections of perishable fabrics with care based on knowledge. One excellent reference is Patsy Orlofsy's "The Collector's Guide for the Care of Quilts in the Home," in *The Quilt Digest 2*.

If you are interested in making a quilt but insecure about your skills or the time you have to devote, there is no better project than a doll-size or crib-size piece. Finishing a small quilt is a goal that can be met in a weekend. You don't need a big frame or the support of a quilting bee; the quilt can be worked on your lap. Before beginning a project inspired by one of these quilts, be sure to familiarize yourself with the General Directions section starting on page 137.

We no longer make quilts just to keep us warm. We continue the tradition for that same sense of pride that our grandmothers and great-grandmothers felt from their handiwork. It is most satisfying to design a quilt of your own. To begin, look at these quilts, and as many others as you can find, to discover which ones you like. Consider which design elements make those quilts appealing to you: the colors, shapes, rhythms, and graphics. Then try to combine these elements in a way that is different than what has come before. It is important to avoid duplicating what has already been done. The black-and-white photos in this book may help you mentally erase the colors that were originally used, so that you may visualize a design in a color palette of your choice. With some thought and planning, you can infuse your design with your own aesthetics and sensibilities and experience the pleasure of creating a highly personal and original work.

I am sure that most if not all of the quilts in this book were made by amateurs. Judging from the length and unevenness of their quilting stitches, it appears that some of the quilts were made by children just learning to sew, or older women whose hands were no longer nimble. Many of these quilts were pieced and even quilted with sewing machines. Many were made from the contents of the scrapbag, rather than from a carefully planned and purchased palette of fabrics. Many are in less than mint condition, showing signs of fading, mildew, acid burns, frayed bindings, or quilting stitches that have come loose.

What makes these little quilts great? Aesthetics is a set of personal choices. By my standards, these little quilts possess many elements of good design: exciting color juxtapositions, strong graphic power, a sense of movement and dimension, and interesting rhythms generated by the repetition of motifs. Their whimsy and sentimentality are the credentials for great folk art. As folk art, their imperfections make them all the more charming. As for those pieces stitched and quilted by machine, they are far from inferior but rather some of the most exciting and impulsively rich designs. For all of these quilts, the patina of time adds value and significance. By all the criteria used to judge art, folk art, and antiques, these are great little masterworks.

By connecting pieces of fabric into crib and doll-bed covers, women were connecting themselves to the generation of quilters before them and to future generations. They used the skills taught by their mothers and grandmothers to strengthen and expand a strong folk tradition. Through hands, hearts, and minds, they put a part of themselves into these quilts, gifts for baby and child, to be handed down to *their* children. The little quilts of yesterday record the most tender and personal stories of women's history in America. It is a rich legacy for all who cherish quilts and for those who continue the tradition of quiltmaking.

Chapter 1: Basics

The simplest patterns often produce the most exciting and sophisticated effects. Designs pieced from squares—or patches based on the square—are an elemental form of quiltmaking. When multiplied, the humble squares become a grid of building blocks. The grid then provides a simple device for juxtaposing colors, as well as a framework for complex graphics.

The simplest quilt in this book and probably my favorite is the Amish One-Patch (Lancaster County, Pennsylvania, c. 1910). As a product of this austere religious community, it was certainly not intended to be hung as a work of art. Perhaps it was made to cover a doll's bed, top a crib for Sunday visitors, or come between an infant and the hard floor; the Amish rarely used even a scatter rug. This one-patch quilt is entirely machine-stitched and without a filling. Nevertheless, an ingenuous and instinctive feel for color made this quilter an artist.

Many quilts such as the Amish One-Patch seem to imitate modern paintings. Characteristics such as bold, flat areas of color, strong lines and diagonals, the way quilt tops are "framed" with borders—are all mirrored in paintings. The vegetable-dyed wools here are as luminous, warm, and unusual as any mixture of artist's paints. When I first saw this quilt, I was immediately reminded of the geometric masterpieces by the abstract painter Paul Klee. In fact, he called this series of his paintings "Magic Squares." They, however, were painted at least fifteen years later. To my mind, quilts have served as an inspiration for modern paintings more often than paintings have influenced quilts.

While the Amish allowed only solid fabrics to be used (prints were considered too gay), the more worldly Mennonites were less restricted. Close inspection of the Checkerboard quilt (Mennonite, c. 1880), reveals the paisley design, nicely scaled for a smaller piece, in the border. Obviously, the quilter wanted her doll-bed cover to be rectangular, for, after close inspection, the checkerboard is one row too large for use as a gameboard. Although not geometrically correct, this little quilt still delivers in a glance all the fun of a lively checkers match.

Piecing four-patch blocks (four squares forming a larger square) makes the one hundred and fifty squares in the Postage Stamp quilt a more manageable endeavor. A square space is left at each bottom corner to accommodate a four-poster doll bed, but the resulting shape, when hung, calls to

Amish One-Patch. c. 1910. 23½" x 31".
Courtesy of Quilts of America, Inc.

mind a doll's kimono. In keeping with the faded, rustic quality of this 1860's piece, I mounted it with a sawed-off yardstick slipped through a casing and suspended it with jute.

The nine-patch is a very popular multiple square unit, composed of a block of three horizontal by three vertical squares. The Nine-Patch Crib Quilt (c. 1920) is as perky as a flower garden, but the plain blocks and borders keep it orderly and contained. Less labor but no less charm is evident in the small, machine-stitched Nine-Patch Doll Quilt (c. 1930). The colors pink, yellow, and blue in the stripping, when combined with its small scale, make this nine-patch quilt cheerful and appropriate for a baby.

You may have to hunt for the nine-patch blocks, but they still predominate in the Irish Chain Variation and Jacob's Ladder crib quilts, shown together over twin beds. Like the first quilt in this chapter, these are also Amish from about 1910. In the Irish Chain, nine-patches combine with rectangles the length of three squares to create a diamond grid cut with crosses. Piecing is evident in some of the blue patches, probably indicating a shortage of fabric on hand. Somber black intensifies the blue and lavender hues to an elegant effect. The color combination and pattern in the Jacob's Ladder quilt is just as riveting. A narrow turquoise border complements the watermelon red and Amish black. In this pattern block, called Road to California outside the Amish community, four-patch units combine with half-squares, or right triangles, to create the nine-patch variation. The blocks are turned in different directions, a veritable tour de force. Beautiful hand-quilting includes a radiant star where the four-patch units from four different blocks come together and an undulating flower-and-vine pattern around the borders. Even though appliqué and printed fabrics were eschewed for their gaiety, lively graphics still found their way into this and many other Amish quilts. Fine workmanship on both of these quilts reflects the discipline of Amish life, as well as the love and respect the Amish felt toward their children.

It was not just within the Amish community that women dressed their children like miniature adults and made crib quilts that were simply miniatures of full-size quilts. This attitude and practice prevailed throughout most of this country up until the early twentieth century. Classic patterns were almost invariably used for doll and crib quilts until a deluge of juvenile themes for bed coverings appeared in the 1930s. What makes these quilts great is that the classic square, one-patch, four-patch, and nine-patch are scaled down in proportion for a smaller-size version. They are intended as small quilts, not fragments cut down from bigger pieces. They succeed as autonomous works of art and demonstrate how simple building blocks can produce complex artistic triumphs.

Amish One-Patch

SIZE: 23" x 30½"

FABRICS: 1 yard for outer border and backing; ⅜ yard for inner border; scraps of assorted colors (up to 54) for patches.

NOTES: Cotton and wool are both used in the antique, which is pieced and quilted by machine. There is no filling, and quilt is bound with the backing.

PATCHES: Make a 2½" square template, and use to cut 54 patches, varying colors.

QUILT TOP: Arrange patches in 6 rows of 9. Sew together. *BORDERS:* Make inner border 1¾" wide. Join to sides (shorter edges), then to top and bottom of quilt top. Make outer border 2" wide. Join as for inner border.

ASSEMBLY AND QUILTING: Mark diagonally through center of all patches in both directions; continue diagonal lines over the borders. In corners of quilt top, continue diagonal markings to complete the grid pattern.

   Cut the backing 1" larger all around, assemble layers, and quilt.

FINISHING: Bind quilt with the backing, making a ½" binding.

Checkerboard

SIZE: 12½" x 13¾"

FABRICS: ⅜ yard for backing, patches, and binding; small amounts contrast color for patches and third color for border.

NOTES: Simple but striking doll quilt is hand-pieced and hand-quilted. Quilting shrinks the dimensions of the squares and quilt overall. Though the directions below echo this quilt's arrangement, you may wish to adapt the design for gameboard use: Place 8 squares on each side—and keep a bag of 1" buttons handy for playing pieces.

PATCHES: Make a 1¼" square template and use to cut 36 squares from each of 2 contrasting fabrics.
QUILT TOP: Arrange squares in a checkerboard pattern as shown in photo. Stitch together in rows; stitch rows together. Add a 1" border, mitering corners.
ASSEMBLY AND QUILTING: Cut backing and batting; assemble quilt layers. Quilt around each square, ⅛" inside seams.
FINISHING: Add a separate ¼" binding.

Checkerboard. c. 1880. 11½″ x 13¼″.
Collection of Sharon L. Eisenstat

Postage Stamp. c. 1860. 19″ square.
Collection of Pat Long Gardner

Postage Stamp

SIZE: 19¾" x 18⅜"

FABRICS: 20" square for backing; scraps of assorted prints for patches.

NOTES: Made for a doll bed, hand-sewn coverlet has no filling. Intended for a miniature four-poster, a square space is left at the two bottom corners, enabling the cover to fit around the posts and hang evenly at the sides and end of the bed. A diagonal quilting grid is unfinished or worn away on the original.

PATCHES: Make a 1⅜"-square template and use to cut 150 squares from assorted fabrics.

QUILT TOP: Sew dissimilar squares together into 75 pairs. Stitch 7 pairs into a row which is 1 patch wide by 14 patches long. Stitch all remaining pairs into four-patch blocks; note that most of these blocks repeat the same 2 fabrics diagonally. Refer to the diagram and arrange four-patch blocks into 3 rows of 7, and position under the first row. Arrange remaining four-patch blocks into 2 rows of 3, and center under the others. Switch blocks around until you are pleased with the overall color pattern, then stitch quilt top together.

ASSEMBLY AND QUILTING: Cut the backing; assemble quilt layers. If desired, insert flannel for filling. Quilt diagonally across four-patch blocks in both directions, extending the diagonals into the top row of single blocks.

FINISHING: Add a separate ¼" binding (here, binding is pieced from different fabrics).

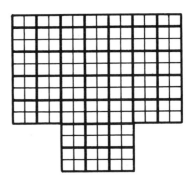

Diagram for Quilt Top

QUILT TOP: Alternate nine-patch blocks and sashing strips in 4 vertical rows, as shown in the diagram. Make 3 stripping bars 1⅜″ wide and place between rows.
BORDERS: Make side borders 2″ wide, top and bottom borders 1¼″ wide.
ASSEMBLY: For backing, cut a rectangle of fabric the same size as quilt top. Pin quilt top and backing together right sides facing. Stitch all around, leaving an opening for turning. Trim corners, turn to right side, and use a pin to prod out corners. Turn open edges to inside; press edges. Topstitch all around, ⅛″ from edge.

Nine-Patch Doll Quilt

SIZE: 18¼″ x 20⅛″

FABRICS: 22″ square for backing, scraps of assorted solids and prints.

NOTES: Pieced quilt separates nine-patch blocks with horizontal sashing and vertical stripping bars. The original is entirely machine-sewn and has no filling.

PATCHES: Make templates: a 1″ square and a ¾″ x 3″ rectangle (sashing strip). Use square template to cut 144 patches from print fabrics, cutting them in groups of 5 or 4 from the same fabric. Use the rectangular template to cut 20 sashing strips from one solid fabric.
QUILT BLOCK (Make 16): Arrange square patches into nine-patch blocks as shown in the diagram; use a group of 5 same-fabric patches for the corners and center of each block, a group of 4 from another fabric for the remaining squares.

Nine-Patch Block

Diagram for Quilt Top

Nine-Patch Doll Quilt. c. 1930. 18¼″ x 20⅛″. Collection of Pat Long Gardner

Opposite: *Nine-Patch Crib Quilt.*
c. 1920. 42″ x 43″. Courtesy of Laura
Fisher/antique quilts and Americana

Nine-Patch Crib Quilt

SIZE: 42¾″ square

FABRICS: 1⅜ yards for backing, 1 yard for plain blocks, ½ yard each of 2 fabrics for borders, scraps of assorted prints.

NOTES: Pieced quilt alternates nine-patch blocks with plain blocks, and sets them on point. Solid borders frame the large square, and hand-quilting emphasizes the block.

PATCHES: Make templates: a 1¼″ square (patch) and a 3¾″ square (block). Use patch template to cut 324 patches from print fabrics, cutting them in groups of 5 or 4 from the same fabric.

QUILT BLOCKS: Arrange square patches into 36 nine-patch blocks as shown in the diagram; use same-fabric patches for the corners and center of each block, another fabric for the remaining squares. For plain blocks, use block template to cut 49 blocks from one fabric.

QUILT TOP: Arrange plain blocks and nine-patch blocks as shown in diagram. Stitch together in horizontal rows, then stitch rows together. Mark outline to set on point, and trim edges. *BORDERS:* Make inner border 2½″ wide. Make outer border 2⅞″ wide.

ASSEMBLY AND QUILTING: Cut backing and batting; assemble quilt layers. Quilt along patches 1/16″ to one side of seams, continuing lines of stitches to create a 1″ diagonal grid over plain blocks and borders.

FINISHING: Using same fabric as inner border, add a separate ⅜″ binding.

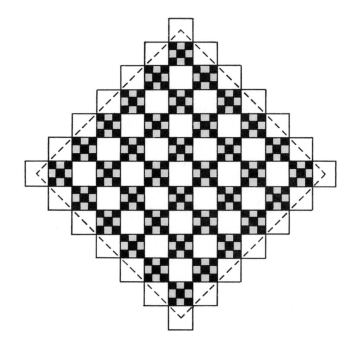

Diagram for Quilt Top

Nine-Patch Block

20

Amish Irish Chain

SIZE: 35¾″ square

FABRICS: 1¼ yards for backing, 1 yard each dark and light colors.

NOTES: Pieced quilt combines nine-patch blocks with plain blocks and rectangles, and sets them on point. Dark and light borders surround the square center.

PATCHES: Make templates: a 1⅛″ square (patch), a 3⅜″ square (plain block) and a 3⅜″ x 10⅛″ rectangle. Use patch template to cut 200 patches from light fabric, 160 from dark fabric. Use templates to cut out 18 plain blocks and 9 rectangles from dark fabric.
QUILT BLOCKS: Combine patches into 40 nine-patch blocks; use light fabric at corners and center of each.
QUILT TOP: Arrange nine-patch blocks, plain blocks, and plain rectangles as shown in diagram. Stitch together in horizontal rows, then stitch rows together. Set design on point, as indicated by dash lines in diagram. *BORDERS:* Make inner border 1⅛″ wide, outer border 2¼″ wide.
ASSEMBLY AND QUILTING: Beginning at the center of each side, transfer actual-size quilting pattern over inner and outer borders; center it over the seam between them. Repeat to each corner.

   Cut backing and batting; assemble quilt layers. Quilt diagonally through center of all square blocks in both directions, extending quilting lines into rectangles to form a diagonal grid over patchwork quilt center. Quilt along marked lines on borders.
FINISHING: Bind quilt with the backing.

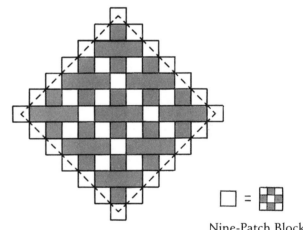

Diagram for Quilt Top

Nine-Patch Block

Actual-Size Quilting Pattern for Border

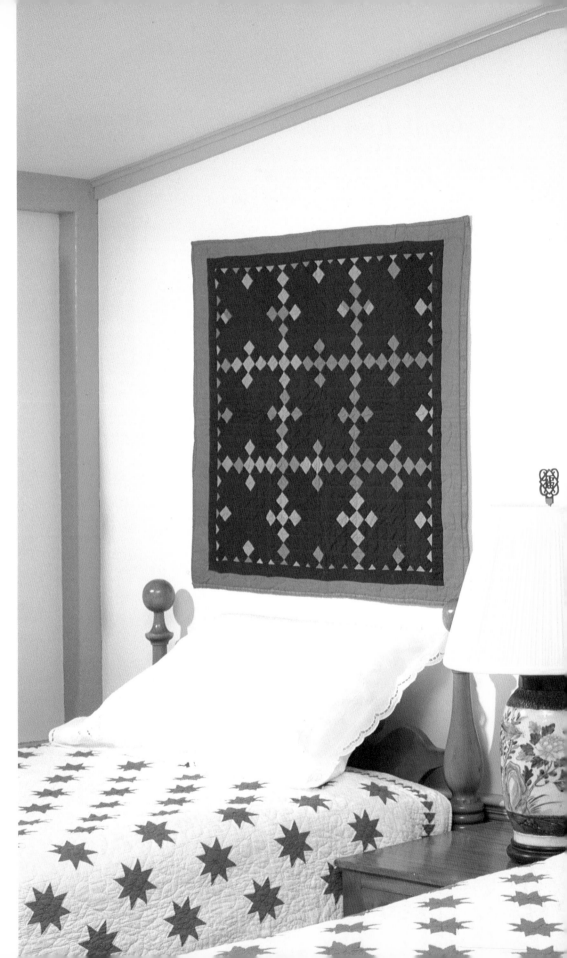

Left: *Amish Irish Chain*. c. 1915.
33¾″ x 35½″. Courtesy of Martha
Jackson Antiques; right: *Jacob's
Ladder*. c. 1910. 32½″ x 39″.
Collection of Ardis B. James

Jacob's Ladder

SIZE: 33" x 39"

FABRICS: 2 yards dark color for patches and backing, 1¼ yards light for patches and outer border, ¼ yard contrast for inner border.

NOTES: Pieced quilt has 20 identical blocks, turned so that "ladders" form diamonds. Within those diamonds, radiant stars are quilted. A vine and tulip design is quilted around the border, and quilt is bound with the backing.

PATCHES: Make templates: a 1" square, a 2" half-square. Use templates to cut 200 square patches and 80 half-square (triangular) patches from both light and dark fabrics.

QUILT BLOCKS: Referring to the diagrams, assemble light and dark squares into 100 four-patch units and light and dark triangles in pairs to form 80 half-square units. For each quilt block, arrange these small blocks as shown in diagram; stitch.

QUILT TOP: Arrange 4 blocks together in a horizontal row. Give second and fourth blocks a quarter turn clockwise; refer to diagram. Repeat to make 5 identical rows. Stack rows vertically. Turn second and fourth rows upside down; stitch rows together.

BORDERS: Make inner border 1¼" wide, outer border 3" wide.

ASSEMBLY AND QUILTING: Enlarge radiant star pattern; center and transfer where 4-patch blocks from 4 different quilt blocks come together to form a square. Pattern shows quilting design for borders; if desired, enlarge to cover width of both borders, then transfer over borders, repeating all around and adjusting to fit.

Cut backing and batting; assemble quilt layers. Quilt radiant stars. Quilt ladders: stitch diagonally through each ladder, ¹⁄₁₆" from either side of center. Quilt along bases of triangles, ¹⁄₁₆" from seams. Quilt borders as suggested or as desired.

FINISHING: Bind quilt with the backing.

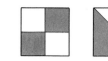

Four-Patch Unit   Half-Square Unit

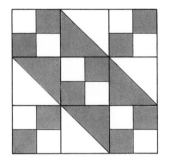

Quilt Block

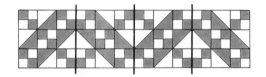

Diagram for Quilt Top: One Horizontal Row

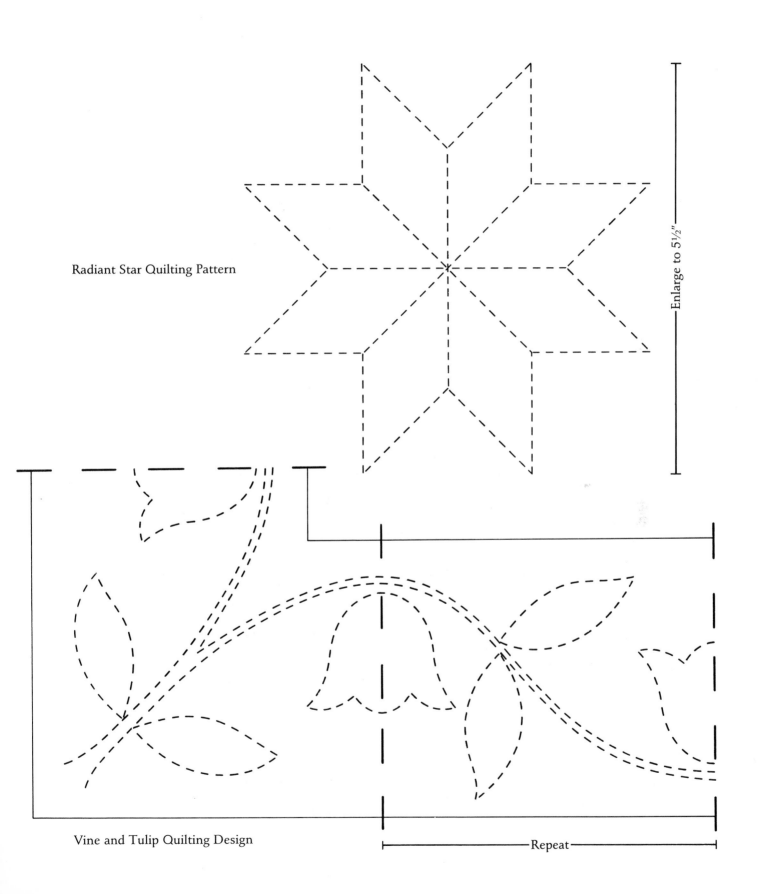

Radiant Star Quilting Pattern

Enlarge to 5½"

Vine and Tulip Quilting Design

Repeat

Chapter 2:   Rhythms

The use and repetition of shapes and colors can make a static composition dance in front of our eyes. Basic shapes—the square, triangle, and circle—inherently suggest different directions in space. Squares and rectangles are essentially horizontal and vertical, but their right-angle, framelike qualities keep a surface locked in and unmoving. Other shapes, however, suggest movement: triangles and diamonds offer strong diagonals—their acute angles point in directions like arrow tips. The circle, on the other hand, implies a continuous spin. By repeating these basic shapes we set up a rhythm, either monotonous or syncopated.

The repetition of color also sets up a rhythm. Warm colors (reds and yellows) seem to advance, while cool colors (blues and greens) seem to recede; repeating certain colors generates a sway or vibration. Many of these quilts have a wonderful sense of movement and rhythm. And because the quilts are small, the eye can easily capture and savor this visual excitement.

In naming a pattern Birds in the Air, or Flying Geese, quilters must have sensed its feeling of movement. Like the quilts in the previous chapter, its elemental quilt block is based on the square. Yet the half-square, or triangle, dominates. The white, triangular geese fly in a triadic formation against a dark night sky. Like many quilts of its era (c. 1880), it has a "devil's eye" or "humility patch": one off-color patch to caution, superstitiously, that only God can create perfection. Interrupting the rhythm set up by the colors, that little rust triangle is a burst of unexpected charm, making imperfection worth coveting.

According to quilt dealer and expert Laura Fisher, the pattern of the next quilt is called Pandora's Box or Pandora's Ribbon. The name endows the quilt with mystery. In this version (c. 1875), strips of diamonds alternate white and printed fabrics, and when joined, create even, horizontal zigzags. The light and dark prints are somewhat random—perhaps due to the fading of some of the patches intended to be dark—so that they syncopate the rhythm. The design on the quilt seems to skip like an erratic electrocardiogram.

If Pandora's Box hints at staccato rhythms, the Honeybee crib quilt evokes a lilting grace. Teardrop "bees" flutter across the borders. Is that the queen bee they are protecting at the center fleur-de-lis? The oak-leaf motif curves as if floating on a breeze. Zigzagging appliqué sets up a quiet pulse of rising and falling rhythm. Contributing to the lightness is the airy, spacious motif of the printed fabric; the motifs are spaced farther apart than in the usual calico selections of its day. From

Birds in the Air. c. 1880. 34" x 42".
Courtesy of Laura Fisher/antique
quilts and Americana

c. 1840, it is probably the oldest quilt in this book, but it is in very good condition. It is also unique among these quilts for being signed by its maker, Jane F. Mesick (inked in one corner). It is thought to have been made in or around Chester County, Pennsylvania.

The quilt with the most unique design in this book is the Strawberries quilt (Lancaster County, c. 1900). The shape and colors of its smaller appliqués uphold this interpretation of its design. Strawberries were a common motif for quilters and were viewed with religious overtones. Used in a threesome, they may have symbolized the Trinity. Having mentioned this, let me say that a great quilt calls up very different, personal associations from everyone who studies it. A science-fiction lover might look at this quilt and see satellites moving around a mother planet. Personally, I am reminded of pillow lace, with bobbins (the hands controlling them unseen) flying around a doily in progress. A puzzling aspect of this quilt is the combination of fastidious hand-appliqué work with machine quilting. This could be the work of two people, each with a different style, possibly working at different dates. Yet the results are exciting: the rigid machine-stitched grid holds the energetic appliqués in check. It also gives the quilt a stiffness that is particularly advantageous for wall hanging.

Borders have become a gauge of good design and an indication that the piece was intended to be an entity unto itself. The Rising Sun quilt (c. 1890), however, lacks a border. The design is naive and the quilting fairly minimal. For these reasons it may not meet most people's criteria for a great little quilt. I respond that its bright colors helped create a cheerful and successful design. Quilters acknowledge how hard it is to piece and appliqué such a neat circle and respect such workmanship. Think of a windmill turning in the breeze, and you will appreciate the illusory movement of this charming piece.

Our eyes and our minds may play tricks on us when we look at these quilts. A variety of optical illusions, kinetics, and colors sets up rhythms for the eye. Historical, pictorial, and emotional associations set up other reverberations in the mind. By always looking just a little different, these designs give never ending pleasure.

$\mathcal{B}$irds in the Air

SIZE: 36½″ x 44″

FABRICS: 1¾ yards dark print for backing, border, and binding; small amounts of assorted prints on a similarly colored dark background; 1 yard white or light color.

NOTES: Crib-size patchwork is based on a nine-patch block that has 6 of the patches divided into dark and light half-squares. The high-contrast pattern, which is the same in each block, uses from 1 to 4 prints with the same color background. A "humility patch" substitutes for one dark patch. Quilt is bordered, then quilted in simple diagonal lines.

PATCHES: Make templates: a 2½″ square, and a 2½″ half-square. For each block (make 20), use the square template to cut 3 patches from dark fabric, and the half-square template to cut 6 patches from same dark fabric, another 6 from light fabric.

QUILT BLOCK: For each block, sew 6 light and dark half-squares together in pairs to form squares. Arrange squares in 3 rows of 3, following diagram for quilt block; sew together.

QUILT TOP: Arrange blocks, all with a dark square patch at upper right corner, in 5 rows of 4. Sew together. *BORDERS:* From dark fabric, make 3″ borders.

ASSEMBLY AND QUILTING: Cut backing and batting; assemble quilt layers. Quilt diagonally across all blocks as indicated on quilt block diagram. Extend this pattern into the border.

FINISHING: Using same fabric as border, make a separate ¼″ binding, and attach.

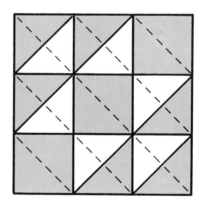

Diagram for Quilt Block

Pandora's Box. c. 1875. 24" x 34". Courtesy of Laura Fisher/antique quilts and Americana

Opposite: *Honeybee.* c. 1840. 39" x 51".
Courtesy of Stella Rubin Antiques

Pandora's Box

SIZE: 28" x 34"

FABRICS: 1⅜ yard for sashing, borders, and backing; ¾ yard white; small amounts of assorted dark prints.

NOTES: Strips of diamonds are joined into blocks, which are set with sashing and stripping. Minimal hand-quilting frames each block.

PATCHES: Make template: trace actual-size diamond pattern. For each block (make 6), cut 50 diamonds from white, 49 from assorted dark prints.

QUILT BLOCK: Refer to strip diagrams and piece diamonds in strips of 9, alternating white and dark print diamonds. For strip I (make 6 per block), begin and end

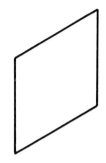

Actual-Size Pattern for Diamond

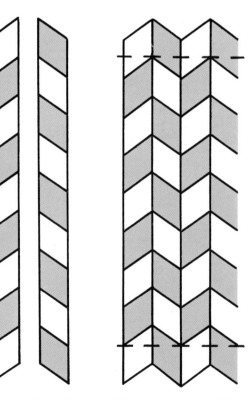

Strip I Strip II   Diagram for Quilt Block

32

with a white diamond. For strip II (make 5 per block), begin and end with a dark diamond. Arrange 11 alternate strips side by side in a herringbone pattern; begin and end with a strip I. Join strips. Refer to quilt block diagram and, on wrong side, draw a line across top of blocks, connecting top points of second diamond in each strip. Trim top of block, leaving seam allowance beyond marked line. Turn block upside down and repeat.

QUILT TOP: SASHING: Make 8 strips 2¾" wide and as long as top edge of quilt block. Sew 1 strip to top edge of each block. Arrange 3 blocks with sashing into a vertical row; sew together. Repeat for second row. Stitch a sashing strip to bottom of each row.

STRIPPING: Make 3 strips 2¾" wide and as long as vertical rows. Arrange strips to alternate with block rows. Sew together.

ASSEMBLY AND QUILTING: Mark lines parallel to sashing and stripping edges; divide each into thirds and continue lines across quilt top in both directions. Cut backing and assemble quilt layers. Quilt along marked lines. Also quilt within each block, stitching ⅟₁₆" to one side of each vertical seam.

FINISHING: Using one of the print fabrics, make a separate ⅜" binding, and attach.

Honeybee

SIZE: 39" x 51½"

FABRICS: 3 yards white for quilt top and backing, 1½ yards contrast color for appliqués.

NOTES: Quilt is appliquéd on sectional white backgrounds, which are then sewn together. Hand-quilting embellishes appliqués and background. Quilt is bound with the backing.

BACKGROUNDS: Make Center 25½" square, two 19½" squares cut diagonally in half for 4 Triangles, and two Borders 6¼" x 38½".

APPLIQUÉS: Make templates: trace, complete, and enlarge patterns as necessary; cut out. Transfer outlines

Diagram for Center

Diagram for Border

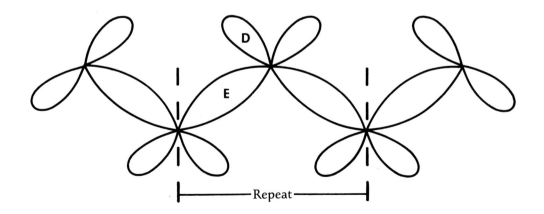

and quilting lines onto contrast fabric as indicated below, and cut out. Do not turn under edges of zigzag appliqués along edges of background pieces, but simply baste close to edge to secure. Pin appliqués to backgrounds so that turned-under edges meet. After arrangement on each background piece is completed, sew pieces in place.

CENTER: Center A on background. Referring to diagram for Center, place a B at each corner of A, then surround each B with 7 C's as shown. Cut a long repeat of zigzags to fit each side; center it. Trim end zigzags slightly to accommodate corner pieces.

TRIANGLES: Use pattern to cut 4 oak leaves. Center 1 on each Triangle, with tip of stem turned toward right angle corner. Do not add zigzags yet.

BORDERS: Cut zigzags to fit short sides and one long (outer) edge of both Borders. Cut 52 D and 24 E. Arrange these pieces as shown in diagram for Border, laying out the repeat 5 times on each and fitting D's over zigzags as shown in photograph.

QUILT TOP: Center and stitch a Triangle to each side of Center. At Center corners, stitch across points of triangles so whole piece lies flat. Add zigzags and corners to perimeter. Stitch Borders to opposite sides.

ASSEMBLY AND QUILTING: If desired, mark background with a diagonal grid. Interrupt these lines for any appliqués. Cut backing and batting; assemble quilt layers. Quilt along marked lines and around each C, D, and E appliqué, ¼" inside edges.

FINISHING: Bind quilt with the backing.

Actual-Size Appliqué Patterns

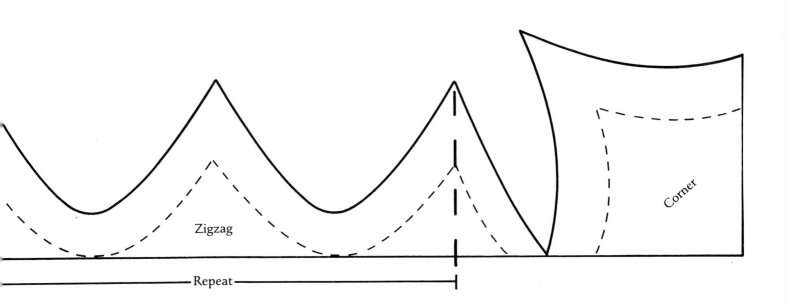

Zigzag

Corner

Repeat

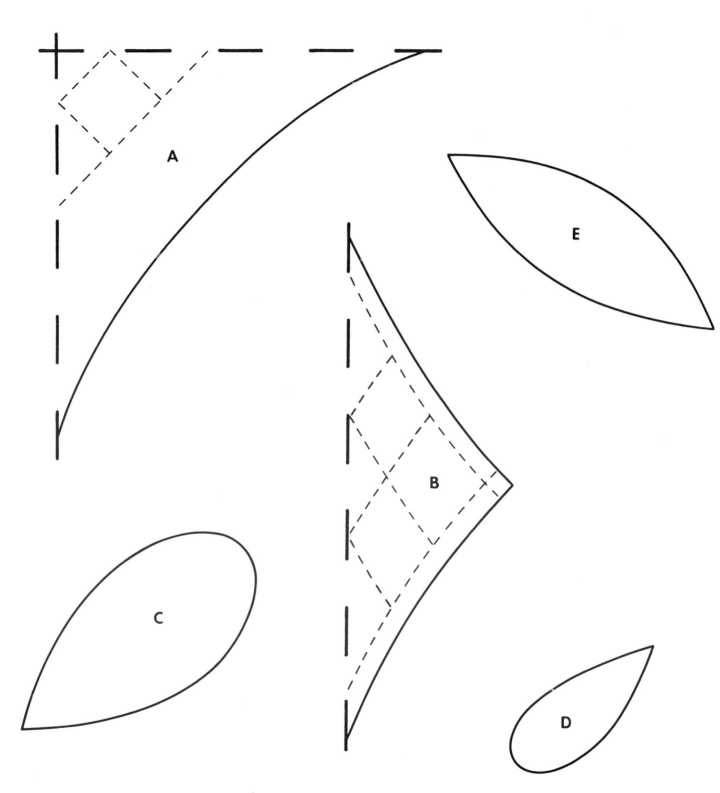

Actual-Size Appliqué Patterns

36

Oak Leaf Appliqué

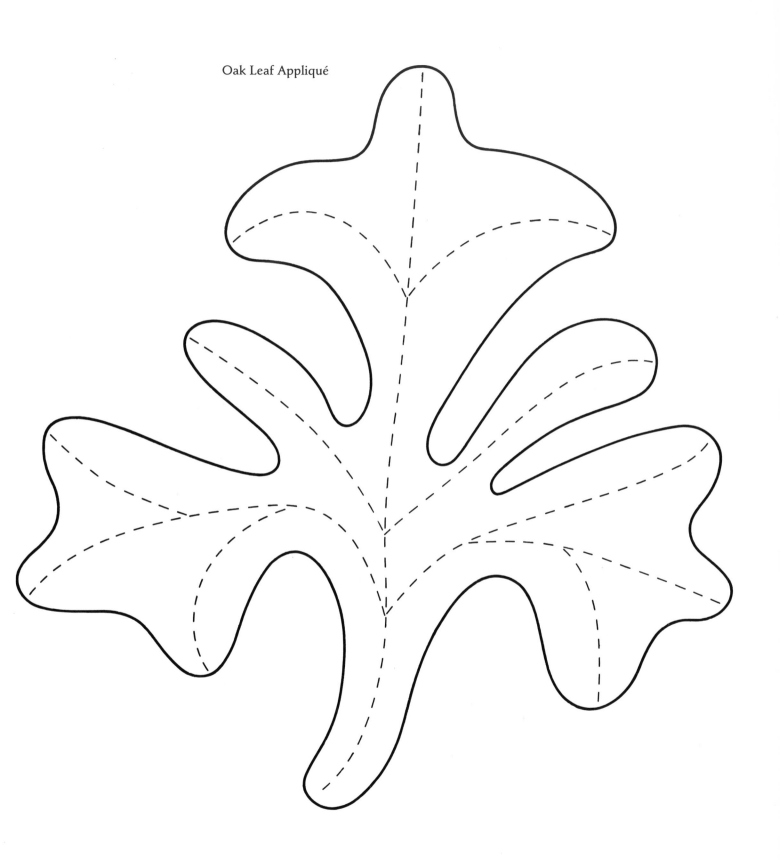

$\mathscr{S}$trawberries

SIZE: 22″ square

FABRICS: ⅝ yard for background and backing; small amounts of several solid colors for appliqués, borders, and binding.
IN ADDITION, YOU WILL NEED: Pearl cotton #8 in contrast color.

NOTES: Center medallion and strawberry shapes are appliquéd on a background; chain-stitch embroidery bridges them. Quilt has two borders and is machine-quilted in an all-over grid.

APPLIQUÉS: Make templates: trace and complete actual-size quarter patterns as necessary; cut out patterns. Cut 1 A and 24 B from one contrast fabric, 24 C from a second contrast fabric. (Note: For oval eyelet openings on A, simply slit the fabric as shown.)
BACKGROUND: From yardage, cut a 17″ square for quilt top background.
QUILT TOP: Center A on background. Draw 3 curvy lines from each peak of A as shown on pattern, and place a C and B at the end of each line. Sew pieces in place. For eyelet openings, clip outward from slit for ⅛″ and turn edges under in a neat oval curve; sew.
EMBROIDERY: With 1 strand of pearl cotton in embroidery needle, chain-stitch along marked lines.
BORDERS: Make 1″ inner border, 1¼″ outer border.
ASSEMBLY AND QUILTING: Mark a 1″ grid of horizontal and vertical lines over entire quilt top. Cut backing and batting, assemble quilt layers, and quilt grid.
FINISHING: Add a separate ¼″ binding.

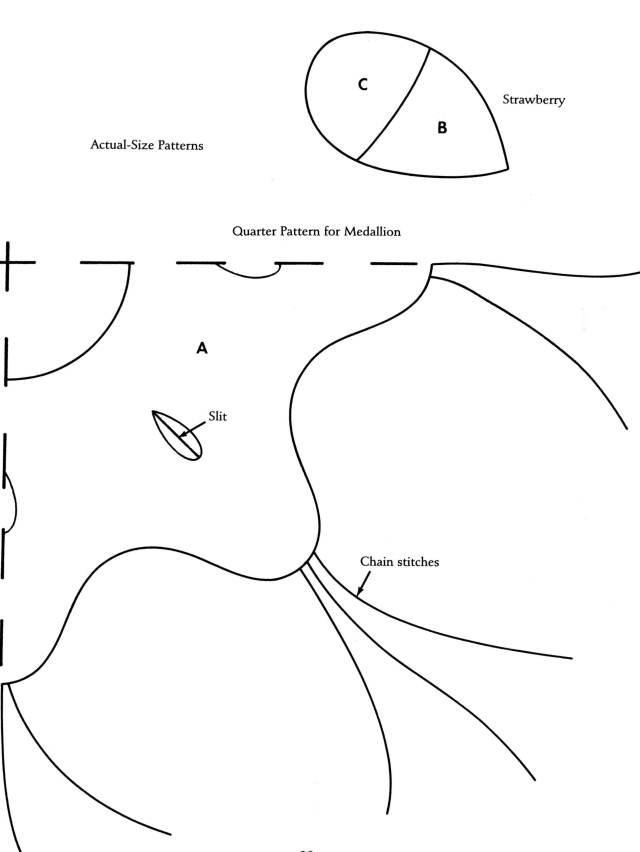

Actual-Size Patterns

Strawberry

C

B

Quarter Pattern for Medallion

A

Slit

Chain stitches

39

Strawberries. c. 1900. 22″ square. Courtesy of Stella Rubin Antiques

Rising Sun. c. 1890. 16″ x 17″. Courtesy of 'all of us americans' folk art

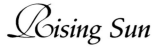 Rising Sun

SIZE: 16½″ square

FABRICS: ½ yard for background, backing, and binding; small amounts of 2 different shades of the same color for appliqués.

NOTES: Shapes are hand-appliquéd on a background, which is then hand-quilted and bound.

BACKGROUND: Cut two 16½″ squares; do not add seam allowance. Set one aside for backing. Fold other in half horizontally and vertically; press folds and open. Trace and transfer actual-size quarter pattern to each quarter.

APPLIQUÉS: Make templates: trace and cut out patterns for A, B, and C. Mark and cut appliqués: cut 1 A and 24 C from darker fabric, 6 B from lighter. Pin to background as marked, alternating B's with background spaces; pin A and C's over B's short edges; add remaining C's.

ASSEMBLY AND QUILTING: Mark for quilting as shown in photograph—a large 12-pointed star plus squares at the corners, or as desired. Cut batting and backing, assemble quilt layers, and quilt.

FINISHING: Using same fabric as background, make a separate ¼″ binding and attach.

Actual-Size Quarter Pattern for Rising Sun

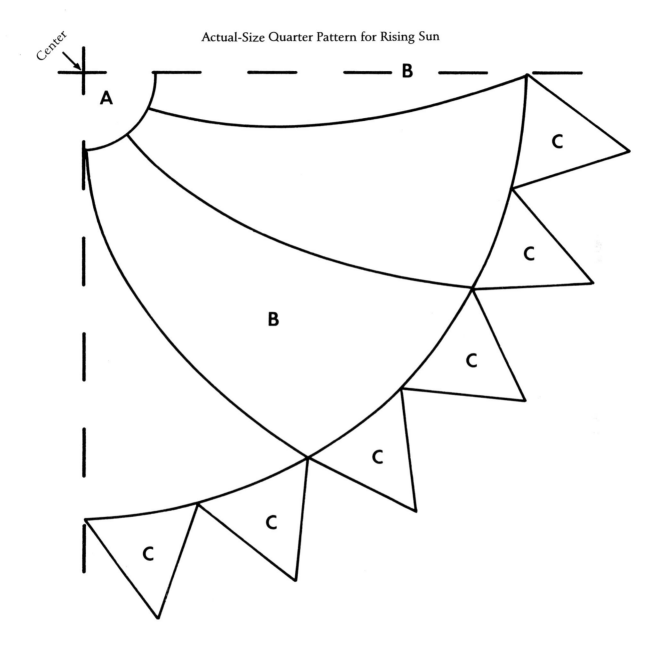

Center

A

B

B

C

C

C

C

C

C

C

43

Chapter 3: Whimsy

There once was a six-legged beetle,
Who made crib quilts: each leg held a needle.
When a quilting bee said,
"Try a large quilt instead,"
She replied, "Gosh, I'm not centipedal!"

Before I go from bad to verse, here is my point: Compared to the large quilt project that loomed almost endlessly ahead of each quilter, the occasional crib or doll quilt must have seemed like a picnic. One could relieve the tedium of the weightier endeavor, which was intended to show off virtuoso stitching skills, by working on a design which simply tickled one's fancy. Small quilts invited spontaneity and experimentation and the result was often a witty, whimsical, and wonderful design.

Illusive motion, as discussed in the previous chapter, is one of the fanciful notions that might have captured the quiltmaker's interest. Ships set sail, pinwheels spin, parasols turn, sunflowers sway, and little urchins stride off in swaggering gaits. Another explanation for the allure of certain designs is that the motifs portrayed are grounded as much in fantasy as in reality. Toys and imagination—as much as real life—inspire themes. Unlikely elements and colors combine for humorous effect.

In the 1800s, while girls developed the proficiency to use a needle, boys learned how to use a jackknife. Boys probably started carving ships to sail in puddles, ponds, or gutters, thereby inspiring the motif sewn by girls. In this 1920s version of Ships, a popular pattern, an aqua pin-dot fleet sails on a white sea. I find this pattern far more effective in miniature than in its full-size renditions. Horizontal stripping forms the sea; it is quilted in very random, loopy curves, as opposed to the precise handling of the rest of the quilt, and the neat, sawtooth border. Those waves, which I doubt would have been done the same way on a large piece, roll out of a spontaneous and intuitive way of working.

Pinwheels were usually available to children of rich and poor families alike, being easy to construct at home of paper, stick, and nail, and widely sold at country fairs. Waving them in the wind provided a quiet recreation approved of even on Sundays. Their quaint charm is celebrated on a square crib quilt, c. 1880. Was the brown gingham left over from a country frock? It is an unexpected but delightful combination with the blue and yellow fabrics. The zigzag border is constructed in an intriguing way, with joined squares and rectangles cocked to one side. If the serious member of a gag team is called the "straight man," and a "straight face" shows no amusement, then zigzags must be the epitome of visual comedy.

Now, if you vote a "straight ticket," you'll find one of the party animals photographed at the top of the stairs your candidate for collecting or incorporating into a quilt. First to come along was the elephant, inspired by Ararat, a beloved old mammoth at the Swope Park Zoo in Kansas City. This mosaic pattern was offered on June 6, 1931, as the regular clip-and-save quilt block design in the *Kansas City Star*. Here, it is followed exactly right down to the choice of colors. The quilter apparently agreed with the accompanying caption: "One thinks of purple and gold . . . because they are royal colors, and in the Far East royalty traveled on elephants." But the quilter gave it an extra, outer border, and this additional framing allowed the creation to stand alone as a quilt rather than merely a quilt block.

Interpreting Ararat as a GOP mascot, the call went out for a Democratic counterpart. Answering the call was the design for "Giddap" the donkey, published in the *Star* seven weeks later on July 22, 1931. Bear in mind that a campaign was gearing up for the presidential election of 1932, won in an almost nationwide sweep by Democrat Franklin D. Roosevelt against the Republican incumbent Herbert Hoover. That could be the reason why this banner-like quilt was made in a bigger scale than the elephant. And in my search for small quilts, I have found more donkeys than any other mosaic pictorial. The *Star* column suggested Giddap be made in orange with brown contrasts, but the blue donkey rendered here strikes the same funny bone as the proverbial purple cow. Rather than continue the mosaic into the background, its maker ingeniously saved herself time by appliquéing the donkey onto a whole-cloth background. The quilting provides the effect, however, of a total mosaic.

I always envision the Bowtie pattern being stitched up on a whim. This ever-funky neckwear turns modern figures like Dagwood Bumstead, Gene Shalit, and PeeWee Herman into caricatures, and it does the same for the funny little quilt shown on page 49. The quilting stitches are very long and uneven, suggesting that it may have been made by a child. Big polka-dots and candy stripes spark up the fabrics of this doll-size caprice (c. 1915).

Sunbonnet Sue, that profiled lass with the big-brimmed, face-concealing hat, has been so overdone in cloyingly sweet versions that she has become an object of derision. In recent years, the Seamsters Union Local No. 500 of Lawrence, Kansas designed and executed a quilt called "The Sun Sets on Sunbonnet Sue," which was credited as the inspiration for a hilarious passage in the 1986 musical *Quilters*, by Molly Newman and Barbara Damashek. Each quilt block of the Union's quilt portrays Sunbonnet Sue in a different death scene—hanging, stabbing, drowning, etc. I am among those who would just as soon condemn Sunbonnet Sue to her final resting place. But when I saw the

Two other versions of c. 1930's Donkey quilts

Sunbonnet Ladies in the collection of the Darien Historical Society, I immediately gave her a reprieve. Adapted from a Marie D. Webster pattern in the 1920s or 30s, it is machine appliquéd and quilted. I love the munchkin look of the short, plump ladies, gabbing by the picket fence. The sunflowers worked in appliqué seem to be an original touch—are they decorating those bonnets in a riotous error of proportion, or are they merely growing in a plot behind the fence?

Giving equal time to Sunbonnet Sue's counterpart is a crib quilt featuring Overall Sam, c. 1920. I am of course taken in by his charm, having a little boy named Sam at home. I love the movement in his stride, with one foot taking off, like the freeze frame of a comic-strip figure walking off after getting in the last word. The oversize garb and the gesture of hands shoved deep into pockets, and the French knots that punctuate the shoes, all add up to a great character. Tom Sawyer has nothing on this fellow! A printed fabric cut on the bias separates the blocks with all the jauntiness of a rickrack trim.

Scale contributes substantially to the whimsical feeling of these quilts. A full-size quilt is a much more serious endeavor, and the awe one feels at the amount of work involved often overshadows our ability to enjoy the design. Small quilts give juvenile themes a more endearing format. And since they are not a huge investment in time, the quilter can stand to be a little more daring and try out some unconventional ideas. Likewise, a novice quilter today doesn't need a lot of courage to try out a bit of whimsy on a smaller project.

Ships

SIZE: 29" x 43"

FABRICS: 2¼ yards white for background and backing, ⅝ yard contrast color for ships, ½ yard contrast color for border and binding.

NOTES: Full squares and half-squares are pieced to form a 4-sail ship against a white sea. Rows are pieced without sashing, but stripping separates the rows. Quilt is bordered with sawtooth blocks and is hand-quilted.

PATCHES: Make templates: a 2" square (A), a 2" half-square (B), and a 2" x 4" rectangle (C). For each quilt block (make 15), cut 6 B and 2 C from background color. Cut 2 A and 6 B from contrast fabric.

QUILT BLOCK: Sew unmatched B's together in pairs to form square units. Arrange patches as shown in diagram for quilt block; sew patches into *vertical* rows, then sew rows together.

QUILT TOP: Arrange 3 blocks in a horizontal row; sew together. Repeat to make 4 more rows. From background fabric, cut 4 strips 2" wide and the length of the ship-block rows. Place strips between rows and sew together. *BORDERS:* Use template B to cut 66 patches from both background and contrast fabrics. Sew unmatched half-squares together in pairs to form square units. Arrange pieced square units into 2 rows of 12 and 2 rows of 21. Turn them so that contrast triangle is always in lower right corner; sew together in rows. Stitch shorter borders along top and bottom of quilt, then stitch longer borders to sides. (Borders will be more regular than those in the original quilt.)

ASSEMBLY AND QUILTING: Mark quilt top for quilting: Referring to diagram, mark ship blocks. Stripping is quilted with curvy lines in a vague, rolling design; if you prefer, use a regular sea-waves scallop.

Cut backing and batting; assemble quilt layers. Quilt around each B patch ⅛" inside seams. Quilt remainder as marked.

FINISHING: Using contrast fabric, make a separate ½" binding, and attach.

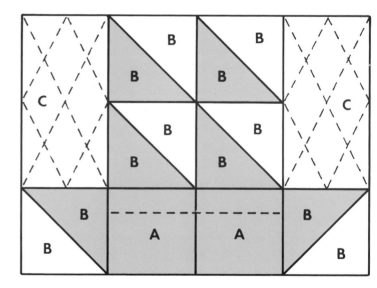

Diagram for Quilt Block

48

Bowtie. c. 1915. 13½" x 17". Courtesy of 'all of us americans' folk art

Pinwheel. c. 1880. 35½" x 38½". Courtesy of Judith and James Milne, Inc.

Bowtie

SIZE: 14" x 16¾"

FABRICS: ¼ yard light, scraps of assorted bright and dark, 17" x 19¾" rectangle for backing.

NOTES: The Bowtie pattern is most easily pieced by hand. This quilt top features 20 blocks. In each block the patches for the bowtie are cut from similar bright or dark fabrics (some faded to light), and the "background" patches are cut from a light fabric. Doll-size piece is quilted with parallel diagonal lines and is bound with the backing.

PATCHES: Make templates: trace actual-size patterns for A and B, as shown on quilt block. For each block (make 20), cut out 2 A's from the same light fabric, 2 A's from the same bright or dark fabric, and 1 B from the same or a similar bright or dark fabric.
QUILT BLOCK: Refer to pattern, and arrange patches. Sew same-fabric A's to opposite sides of B. Sew A's together along their short edges.
QUILT TOP: Arrange blocks into 5 horizontal rows of 4. Sew together. *BORDER:* Add a 1¼"-wide border.
ASSEMBLY AND QUILTING: Cut batting and assemble quilt layers. Quilt diagonally through all bowtie blocks as shown by short dash lines on pattern; extend quilting lines into borders.
FINISHING: Trim backing to ½" larger all around. Bind quilt with the backing.

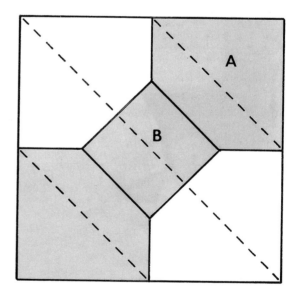

Actual-Size Quilt Block

Pinwheel

SIZE: 34½" square

FABRICS: ⅝ yard light color, ¾ yard medium color, ¼ yard dark color, 1 yard print or fourth color for plain blocks and border, 1 yard for backing, ½ yard for binding.

NOTES: Pinwheel blocks alternate with plain blocks, all set on point. Rectangular and square patches are also set on point to form a zigzag border.

PATCHES: Make templates: trace actual-size pattern for pinwheel block. Make templates for Patches A and B, and also C—the entire square. Use templates to cut 100 A patches from both light and dark fabrics. Cut 100 B patches from medium fabric. Cut 36 C's from a fourth fabric, for plain blocks.

QUILT BLOCK (Make 25): Sew light and dark A patches together in pairs to form square units. Referring to pattern, sew 4 square units together to form pinwheel. Sew a B to each side of the pinwheel, for pinwheel block.

QUILT TOP: Refer to diagram for quilt top to arrange pinwheel blocks (P) and plain blocks. Sew together and

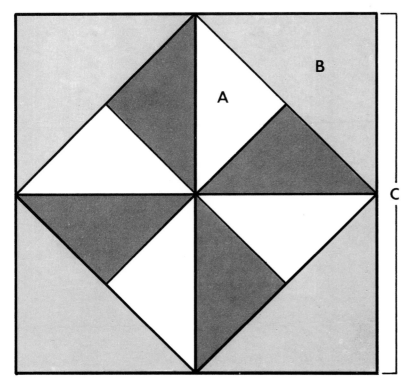

Actual-Size Pattern for Pinwheel Quilt Block

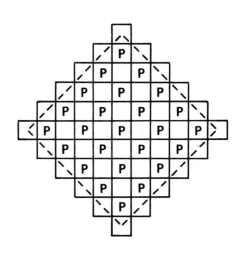

Diagram for Quilt Top
P = Pinwheel Block

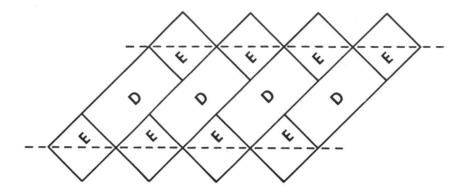

Diagram for Border

set on point. *BORDERS:* Make templates: A 1¾" x 3½" rectangle (D), and a 1¾" square (E). Use D to cut 60 rectangles from same fabric as plain blocks. Use E to cut 120 patches from light fabric. Stitch a square to each short end of each rectangle. Refer to border diagram to assemble borders as follows: Place 14 joined square-rectangle units in a staggered row. Repeat for a second row. Make 2 more rows of 14 square-rectangle units each, but arrange them on the opposite diagonal. Trim zigzag edges as indicated by dash lines on diagram to make 3¾"-wide borders. Stitch matching border strips to opposite edges of quilt top; miter corners.

ASSEMBLY AND QUILTING: Cut backing and batting; assemble quilt layers. Quilt ³⁄₁₆" to inside of seams as follows: For each pinwheel block, quilt around each of the 4 quadrants. On border, quilt in parallel lines along long edges of rectangles, extending stitches into the "square" patches. Quilt along inside edge of border.

FINISHING: Add a separate ¼" binding.

 Sunbonnet Ladies

SIZE: 36″ x 50″

FABRICS: 3 yards for background and backing; ½ yard for border strips; scraps of assorted solids, prints, and checked fabrics.
IN ADDITION, YOU WILL NEED: Scraps of assorted narrow ribbons; white and contrast color sewing thread.

NOTES: Figures and border strips are straight-stitched by machine to background. Quilt is sandwiched with the thinnest of fillers, possibly flannel. Fence design is machine-quilted. Outside edges on actual quilt are turned to the inside and whipstitched, but directions below call for quilt to be sewn together inside out, then turned, to make finishing easier.

BACKGROUND AND BACKING: Mark two 36″ x 50″ rectangles; cut out.
BORDER STRIPS: Make 4 strips 1⅜″ x 36″, 4 strips 1⅜″ x 50″ (piecing as necessary). On each, press seam allowances to wrong side. Arrange strips on background: Place outer strips 1⅜″ from outside seam allowance, inner strips 1⅜″ away, toward center; place strips along both short sides first. Machine-stitch close to folded edges; sew in only one direction on each strip to avoid puckers.
APPLIQUÉS: Make templates: photocopy the actual-size patterns for Sunbonnet Ladies. Cut shapes (adding seam allowances) from desired fabrics for 8 Ladies. Vary dresses and use of sunflowers and parasols. Use narrow ribbon for parasol handle. Refer to the photograph and arrange figures at center of each inner border strip. Machine-stitch all pieces close to turned under edges with white (or matching) thread. Also stitch detail lines, as indicated on patterns by dash lines. Add ribbon trims to embellish an occasional bonnet, waist, or hem.
ASSEMBLY AND QUILTING: Mark for quilting: trace actual-size fence design onto tracing paper, repeating

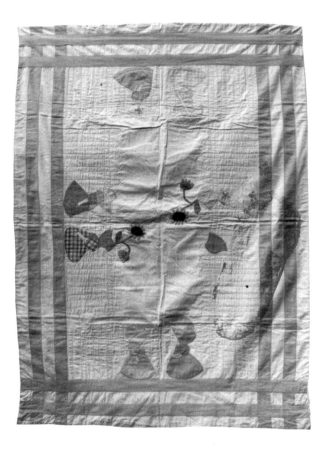

fence posts for a total of 6. Transfer pattern to quilt top as follows: Place fence pattern along short sides of quilt top to either side of Ladies. Transfer only as many posts as will fit. Place pattern along sides of quilt top and transfer as before, stopping repeat so fence ends 1″ from design marked along short edges.

Place quilt top and backing right sides together on top of optional batting or flannel, cut to same size. Stitch around, leaving a 10″ opening. Trim corners and turn quilt to the right side. Turn raw edges to inside and slip-stitch closed. Machine-quilt marked fence, using a contrasting color thread.

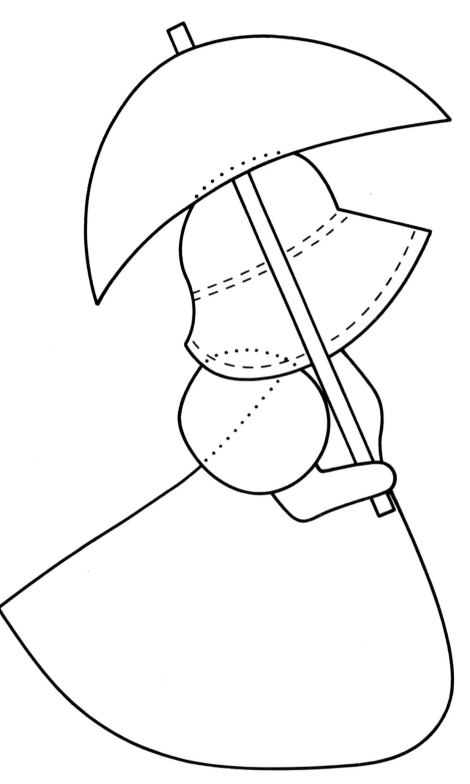

Actual-Size Patterns for Sunbonnet Ladies

54

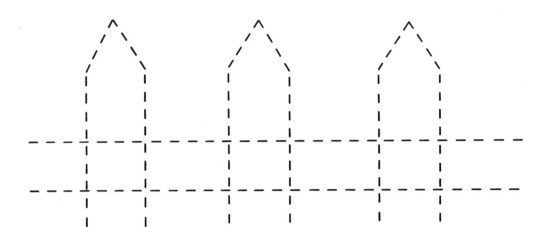

Actual-Size Fence Quilting Design

Sunbonnet Ladies. c. 1930. 36″ x 50″.
Collection of the Darien Historical Society

Overall Sam. c. 1920. 31″ x 54⅜″.
Courtesy of Quilts of America, Inc.

Overall Sam

SIZE: 29½" x 52½"

FABRICS: 3 yards background color for blocks, borders, and backing; 1 yard for stripping (or substitute 9 yards ½"-wide single-fold bias tape), ¼ yard for binding; assorted fabric scraps for appliqués.
IN ADDITION, YOU WILL NEED: One skein of white 6-strand embroidery floss.

NOTES: Figures are appliquéd onto rectangular blocks, which are then joined. After a border is added, bias strips cover all seams. Blocks are quilted with a simple grid, borders with a chain-link repeat, corners with a leaf.

QUILT BLOCK (Make 12): From background fabric, mark 7" x 11" rectangles; cut out. Mark a 6" x 9" rectangle centered on block. Mark inner rectangle in a grid of 1" squares.
APPLIQUÉS: Make templates: trace actual-size pattern for Overall Sam. Cut all hats, sleeves, shoes from one fabric. Cut hatband, overall, cuff from one fabric, but vary the fabrics so blocks are not all the same. Arrange figure on the center of each block, pinning down pieces in this order: shoes, overalls, hat, hatband, sleeve, cuff. Sew pieces in place. Use 3 strands of embroidery floss to make French knot "buttons" on each shoe where indicated on pattern by small circles.
QUILT TOP: Arrange blocks in 4 rows of 3. Sew blocks together in rows, then sew rows together. *BORDERS:* Using background fabric, make 3¾" borders. *TRIM:* Make ½"-wide strips cut on the bias and press seam allowances to wrong side. Pin strips to quilt top, centering them over seams; first cover horizontal seams, then vertical. Slip-stitch along both edges of all strips.
ASSEMBLY AND QUILTING: Mark quilting design on borders: use diagram as a general guide but work freehand and draw a leaf in each corner, chain links along each side.

Cut backing and batting, assemble quilt layers, and quilt on marked lines.
FINISHING: Add a separate ½" binding.

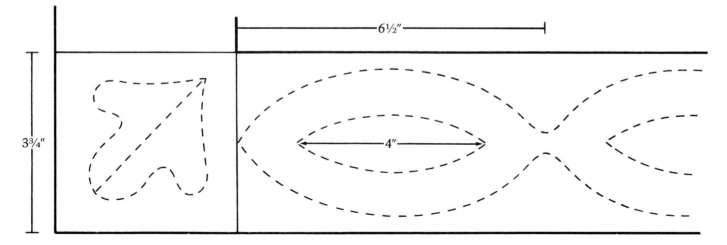

Quilting Diagram for Border

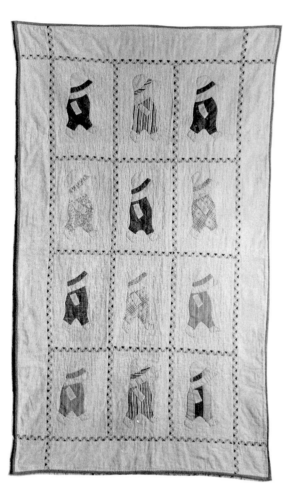

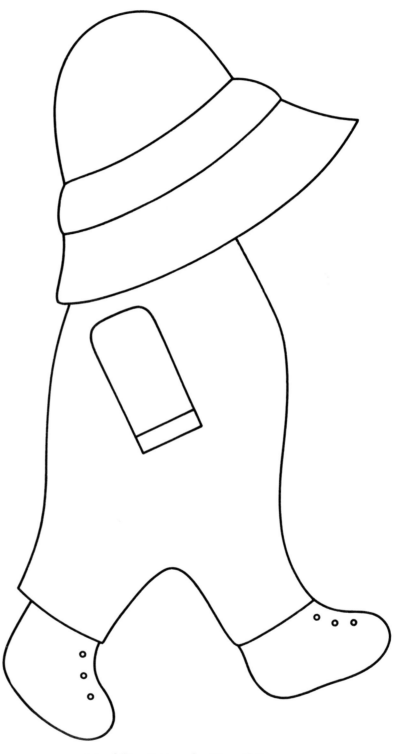

Actual-Size Pattern for Overall Sam

Left: *Donkey.* c. 1930. 27½" x 25".
Courtesy of Cathy Smith antique
quilts; right: *Elephant.* c. 1930.
25½" x 18". Courtesy of Cathy Smith
antique quilts

Donkey

SIZE: 27½" x 25"

FABRICS: 1 yard for background and binding, ¾ yard for backing, ¼ yard for donkey body, ⅛ yard for contrast, scrap of white for eye.

NOTES: Donkey body is a mosaic of squares and half-squares, which is appliquéd onto a whole-cloth background. Quilting extends the grid over the background.

PATCHES: Make templates: a 1⅝" square and half-square. From fabric for donkey body, cut 46 squares and 29 half-squares. From contrast fabric cut 4 squares and 19 half-squares. From white, cut 1 half-square.

QUILT TOP: Refer to chart and arrange squares and half-squares. Sew half-squares together to form squares wherever possible. Sew patches into horizontal rows and sew rows together.

Cut out a 27½" x 25" rectangle from both background fabric and backing fabric; do not add seam allowance. Center donkey mosaic on background; appliqué in place.

ASSEMBLY AND QUILTING: Mark quilt top: extend seam lines of mosaic onto background, continuing grid over the entire surface. Cut batting and assemble quilt layers. Quilt in the seams and along the marked lines.

FINISHING: Using same fabric as background, make a separate ¼" binding, and attach.

Chart for Donkey

62

 Elephant

SIZE: 22⅝″ x 16¾″

FABRICS: ½ yard for backing; ⅜ yard each of colors for elephant body and binding, contrast and inner border, background and outer border.

NOTES: Quilt is a mosaic, pieced following a chart. The inner border is made mosaic style, but the outer border is added in strips. Quilting echoes the grid.

PATCHES: Make templates: a 1⅜″ square and half-square. Use template to cut the following: from color for elephant body, 46 squares and 30 half-squares; from contrast color, 7 squares and 23 half-squares, plus 50 squares for inner border; from color for background, 38 squares and 17 half-squares.

QUILT TOP: Refer to the chart and arrange squares and half-squares (including those for inner border). Sew half-squares together in pairs to form squares. Sew squares together in rows, then sew rows together.

OUTER BORDER: Using same color as background, make 1⅜″ outer border; miter corners.

ASSEMBLY AND QUILTING: Cut backing and batting; assemble quilt layers. Quilt close to one side of each seam, extending the lines into outer border.

FINISHING: From same fabric used for elephant body, make a separate 5/16″ binding, and attach.

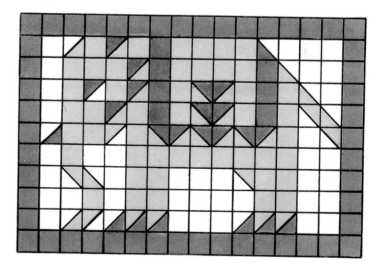

Chart for Elephant

Chapter 4: Sentiment

In the nineteenth century, special patterns or palettes were not reserved for crib and doll quilts. By the 1920s, that changed. Women had won greater equality, and labor-saving devices now eased their domestic drudgery. They no longer needed to bear and raise large families to help with all the work. They felt freer to indulge their sentimental sides. To cater to this trend, a plethora of designs for floral patchwork and appliqué appeared in newspapers and pattern books. Fabric manufacturers supplied a greatly expanded selection of colors and prints. Pastels captivated the public in the 1920s and 30s, when all of the quilts in this chapter were made. Understand, however, that the practice of using pink for girls and blue for boys was not standardized until the mid-1940s.

Baby pink and blue bring sentiment to the Diamonds doll quilt, and quiets its circusy harlequin pattern. The design is intriguing: while it is hard to piece diamond patches, strip-piecing cleverly sidesteps the chore. Quilting stitches superimpose an argyle design. With the side edges following the outline of the diamonds, this quilt must have looked charming on a doll's bed.

Posies Round the Square repeats a block of pink and blue that resembles a child's sweet, simplistic drawing as seen through a kaleidoscope. It combines a Robbing-Peter-to-Pay-Paul patchwork background with appliqué work for the flowers. In doing so, it epitomizes the transition between the historical preference for classic patchwork patterns and the new found popularity of appliqué, with its huge range of pictorial possibilities. The inspiration for this design probably came from versions published in the *Kansas City Star* and *Needlecraft Magazine*'s July 1934 issue.

Rose of Sharon was one of the most widely used quilt patterns for a bride's trousseau. It is one of the oldest appliqué patterns that originated in this country. The flower's mention in the Bible gave it spiritual significance, yet the reference is from a most sensual paean to romantic love in the Song of Songs, 2:1–4:

I am a rose of Sharon,
A lily of the valleys.
As a lily among thorns,
So is my love among the daughters.
As an apple-tree among the trees of the wood,

So is my beloved among the sons.
Under its shadow I delighted to sit,
And its fruit was sweet to my taste.
He hath brought me to the banqueting-house,
And his banner over me is love.

Upper left: *Diamonds.* c. 1930. 23½" x 26½".
Courtesy of 'all of us americans' folk art;
right: *Posies Round the Square.* c. 1930. 28" x 39½".
Courtesy of Laura Fisher/antique quilts and Americana

In this lovely quilt, a garland of roses of Sharon surrounds the word "Baby," rendered in a satin-stitched script. Baby quilts were often made before the baby was born. Without the knowledge of its sex or name, the expectant mother—or one of her relatives—would lovingly write the word "baby" as a welcome to the little stranger soon to arrive.

The Single Wedding Ring, another pattern closely associated with brides, has a strong graphic design. The shape of the ring, like a heavy mill wheel, reminds me of the logo used by a well-known bank. Rendered in more than two colors, the pattern is also known as Crown of Thorns or Georgetown Circle. It is a weighty, angular motif. But the small scale, delicate colors, and quilted network of small circles soften this piece until it is eminently palatable to modern tastes in baby quilts.

Whitework, a white-on-white design, meant the quintessential effort at a "best" quilt. Sandi Fox writes in her book, *Small Endearments: 19th-Century Quilts for Children*, "The all-white quilt . . . was a comprehensive exercise in creative and technical excellence, and the result would be in many ways a measure of personal vanity. . . . The woman who worked the all-white quilt did not want color or pattern to distract the eye from the fineness of her stitch." This small endearment from twentieth-century Pennsylvania fits that description most aptly. The piecework baskets with appliquéd handles and quilted butterflies, all in whitework, must have made its maker proud.

The Iris pattern was offered by Mountain Mist in 1931. But here the quiltmaker applied some changes to her rendition, scaling the design down, and emphasizing the contours of the octagonal blocks by using yellow rather than ecru for those incomplete blocks around the center. Most flower motifs are not as literal as these. Even the lack of planning that cuts off the irises at the top and bottom comes off as charming human error. Subtle shade differences between stems and leaves and the vibrant variety of petal colors create a decorative effect in the Art Nouveau tradition.

Proving that good things come in small packages is the 11¼" square quilt with a wreath of lavender buds. This little piece is one of the humblest and sweetest textiles I have ever seen. Lacking a filling, it may have draped gracefully over a small doll bed.

Throughout American history, women have often considered their children as their best achievements. Making small quilts for the purpose of keeping them warm in their cribs or beds could be accomplished with minimum effort. The fact that they put more effort than was necessary into making quilts pretty was surely a celebration of their "best achievements" as well as their sewing skills. It was a testament of their love and their pride—to be read by their friends, family, and descendants as much as by the child for whom the quilt was intended. Furthermore, in bestowing dolls and doll quilts on their children, women transmitted their values concerning the importance of child-raising in their lives. They also transmitted the incentive to sew and quilt to the next generation.

iamonds

SIZE: 21½″ x 25″

FABRICS: 1⅜ yards white for patches and backing,
¾ yard contrast color for patches and binding, ⅝ yard
second contrast color for patches.

NOTES: Strip piecing constructs 7 horizontal groups of
diamonds, with truncated top and bottom edges, which
are then joined. Sides of the diamonds are kept intact,
producing zigzag edges. Quilting adds an argyle pattern
to the diamonds.

STRIP PIECING: Cut ⅞″-wide strips (add seam
allowances) 32″ long. Seam 5 together: alternate 3 white
with 2 colored strips; always start and end with white.
Repeat, varying the colors, to produce 7 striped
rectangles. Mark a line across rectangles at a 60° angle
so that line is 1″ long across each strip: draw a parallel
line 1″ away. Adding seam allowances, continue to
mark diamonds along joined strip; see cutting diagram.
Refer to the piecing diagram and arrange 22 strips taken
from the various rectangles in rows set on point,
making a harlequin pattern. Remove diamonds from
the lower left side and upper right sides, making a
rectangular shape with zigzag edges. Mark straight
lines across top and bottom as shown on piecing
diagram and cut away points, leaving seam allowances.
Repeat to make 6 more rectangles.

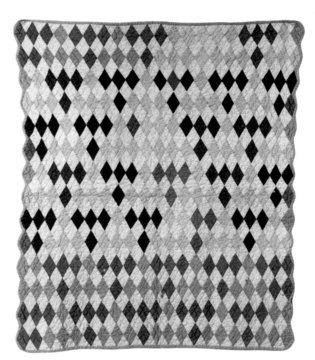

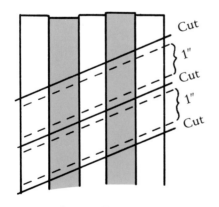

Cutting Diagram

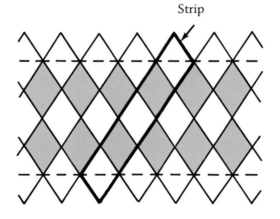

Piecing Diagram

67

QUILT TOP: Arrange the 7 rectangles in a vertical stack. Sew together, matching halves of white diamonds.

ASSEMBLY AND QUILTING: Cut backing and batting; assemble quilt layers. Quilt diagonally through centers of diamonds; see quilting diagram.

FINISHING: Add a separate ¼" bias binding, easing it around the angles on the sides.

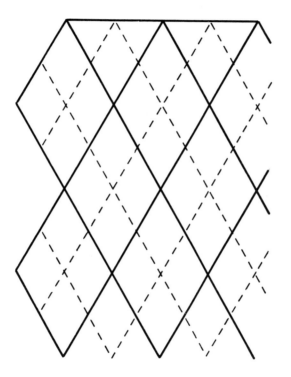

Quilting Diagram

Posies Round the Square

SIZE: 28" x 39"

FABRICS: ⅞ yard for backing, 1 yard for patches and border, ⅝ yard second color for patches, small amounts of 3 colors for posy appliqués.

NOTES: Quilt block combines Rob-Peter-to-Pay-Paul piecework with floral appliquéd triangular patches to make 6 square blocks. They are straight-set; surrounded by a mitered border and bound with the backing. Hand-quilting is modest.

PATCHES: Make templates: trace actual-size patterns for A (completing quarter pattern) and B; make a 5½" half-square for C.

Choose 1 fabric for A patches, another for B and C. For each block (make 6), cut 1 A, 4 B, and 4 C.

APPLIQUÉS: Make templates: trace actual-size pattern for posy and use to cut circles for flower head and flower center, stem, and 2 identical leaves. Refer to the quilt block diagram and arrange a posy on each C. Sew in place.

QUILT BLOCK (Make 6): Sew a B to each side of A, forming a square. Sew a C to each side of square.

QUILT TOP: Arrange blocks in 3 rows of 2. Stitch together in rows, then stitch rows together. BORDERS: Make contrast-color 2½" borders, mitering the corners.

ASSEMBLY AND QUILTING: Cut backing and batting; assemble quilt layers. Quilt from stem to stem across center of A patches in both directions, all around each B patch just inside seams, all around each posy just outside edges, and along leaf centers, for "veins." Quilt along border, dividing it into thirds.

FINISHING: Bind quilt with the backing.

Appliqués

Actual-Size Patterns

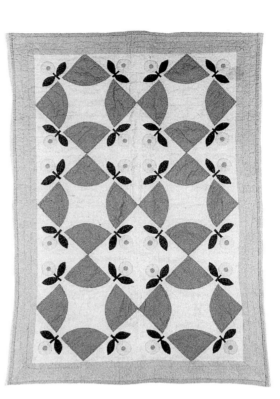

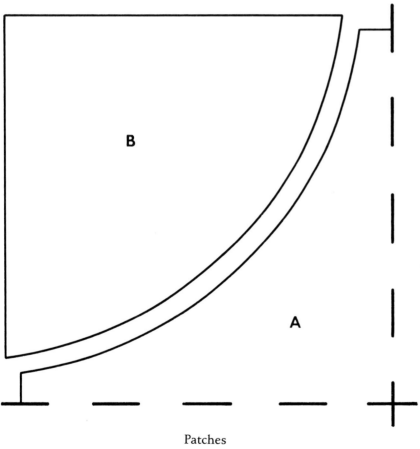

Patches

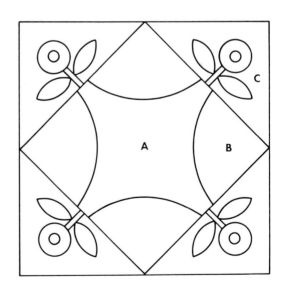

Diagram of Quilt Block

69

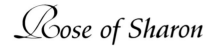

Rose of Sharon

SIZE: 35" x 45"

FABRICS: 2¼ yards for background, outer border, and backing; ½ yard medium shade for flowers and inner border, small amounts of dark and light shades, plus 1 color for vine, leaves, and calyses of buds.

IN ADDITION, YOU WILL NEED: 6-strand embroidery floss to match background fabric, or as desired.

NOTES: Crib quilt features an appliquéd garland of blossoms, buds, and leaves, surrounding the word "Baby" embroidered in satin stitch. The wide outer border acts as a binding, framing both sides of the quilt. A grid of quilting stitches provides the finishing.

├──────────────── Enlarge to 11" across ────────────────┤

Rose of Sharon. c. 1920. 35" x 45".
Courtesy of Stella Rubin Antiques

APPLIQUÉS: VINE: Cut a bias strip 1¼″ wide and 44″ long (this includes seam allowance). Press under seam allowance on either side so that strip is ½″ wide; for last 6″ of strip press under less so strip broadens to 3/4″ wide. *FLOWERS AND LEAVES:* Make templates: trace individual pattern shapes A through F and use to cut appliqués as follows:
BLOSSOMS (Make 4): Cut A petals in 1 piece, B petals individually and C in 1 piece. Cut A's, B's and C's each from a different fabric, shading from dark to light.
BUDS (Make 5): Cut some D buds from medium shade of fabric, some from dark. Cut all E calyses from vine fabric. *LEAVES* (Make 8): Cut from vine fabric.
QUILT TOP: For background, make a rectangle 23″ x 28″. *BORDERS:* Make a 3¼″ inner border. For outer border, which folds to the back as a wide binding, use same fabric as background. Make strips 10½″ wide for top and bottom of quilt top, 5½″ wide for the sides.

Refer to the photograph and mark an 18″ diameter three-quarter circle on center of background. Place bias vine strip over it, with wider end at lower left center. Assemble blossoms; quilt across center of A through all layers. Place blossoms on vine as shown; cut off any excess vine. Place buds and leaves with ends tucked under vine. Sew all pieces in place.
EMBROIDERY: Take pattern for lettering to your local photocopy center and have pattern enlarged to a 11″ length. Or, design lettering for a name of your choice which will fit the center area nicely. Transfer lettering to center of garland. Using 3 strands of floss in embroidery needle, work all single lines in stem stitches, and fill in all double lines with horizontal satin stitches.
ASSEMBLY AND QUILTING: Press under seam allowance on outer borders and fold them lengthwise in half. Mark a 1″ diagonal grid over quilt top interrupting grid for lettering and appliqués. Cut batting and backing to fit within fold lines. Assemble quilt layers, slipping batting and backing under folded borders. Pin border edges to backing; slip-stitch to secure. Quilt each blossom just outside tier of B petals. Quilt along marked lines.

Leaf

D

Bud

E

Blossom

C

B

A

Actual-Size Appliqué Patterns

73

Left: *Whitework.* c. 1930. 20″ x 27″. Courtesy of 'all of us americans' folk art; right: *Single Wedding Ring.* c. 1930. 27⅜″ x 35½″. Collection of the author, courtesy of Yankee Doodle Dandy

Whitework

SIZE: 19⅛″ x 24¾″

FABRICS: 1¼ yards of solid color fabric: a polished cotton shows off the quilting beautifully.

NOTES: Doll-size quilt alternates pieced blocks—the classic basket with appliquéd handle—and plain blocks. The setting is on point, with border all around. Quilting adds butterflies to whole plain blocks, concentric triangles (which echo the shapes of basket patches and partial plain blocks), and zigzags along the border.

PATCHES: Make templates: trace actual-size pattern for pieces A through F and also the entire 4″ square. Note that E is a large triangle with F superimposed on it.
PLAIN BLOCKS: Use 4″-square template to cut 20 plain blocks.
BASKET BLOCKS: For each block (make 12), cut 2 A, 2 B, and 1 each C, D, E, and F. Join an A to each B, seam each to short sides of C. Add D. Appliqué F to center of E, then join the two half-squares to complete block.
QUILT TOP: Refer to diagram and arrange rows of plain blocks and basket blocks. Sew together in rows, then sew rows together. Set on point, as indicated by dash lines. *BORDERS:* Add a ⅞″ border, mitering corners.

ASSEMBLY AND QUILTING: Transfer actual-size butterfly pattern to whole plain blocks. Mark concentric triangles ¼″ apart on half and quarter plain blocks, and on C, B, and D patches of basket blocks. Plan and mark a zigzag along borders. Cut backing and batting; assemble quilt layers. Quilt along marked lines. Also quilt ⅛″ inside edges of butterfly blocks and A and E patches. Quilt on E patches ¼″ inside basket handles.
FINISHING: Using same fabric, make a separate ¼″ binding, and attach.

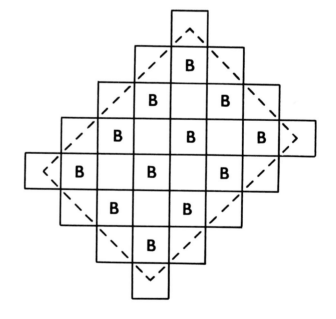

Quilt Top Diagram
B = Basket Block

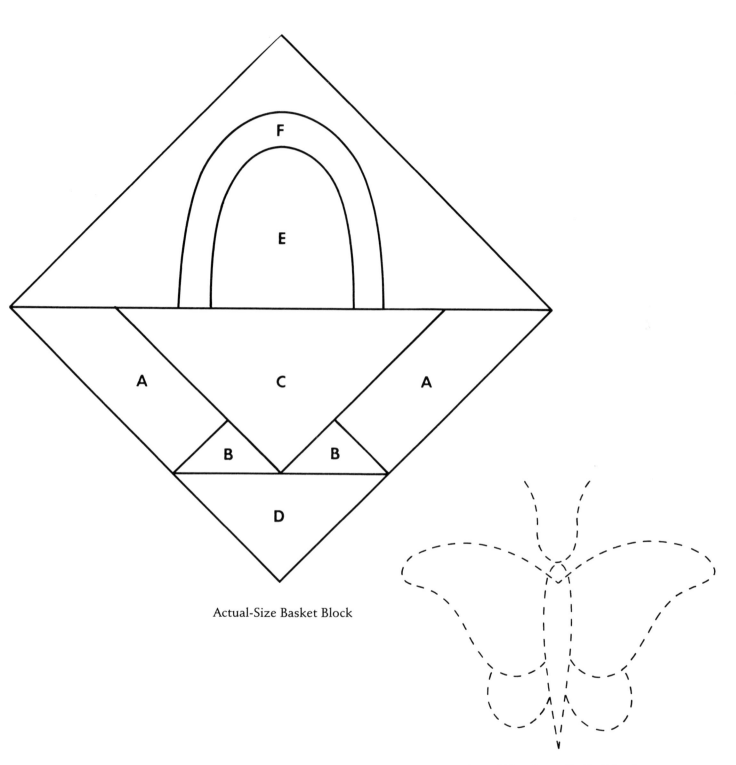

Actual-Size Basket Block

Actual-Size Butterfly Quilting Pattern

QUILT BLOCK (Make 12): Sew unmatched half-squares together in pairs to form squares. Follow diagram to arrange squares; sew together in rows, then sew rows together.

QUILT TOP: Arrange quilt blocks in 4 rows of 3.

BORDER: Add 1½" border, mitering corners.

ASSEMBLY AND QUILTING: Make a template for a 2½" circle. Refer to quilting diagram and use template to make overlapping circles over entire surface. Cut backing and batting; assemble quilt layers. Quilt on marked lines.

FINISHING: Make a separate ⅜" binding and stitch to quilt top. Fold all of binding over onto backing; slip-stitch in place.

Single Wedding Ring

SIZE: 27⅜" x 35½"

FABRICS: 2 yards of 1 color for patches, backing, and border; 1½ yards of contrast color for patches and binding.

NOTES: This classic piecework pattern is based on a square block with 25 equal sections arranged in 5 rows of 5. Center rows are square patches, all others are joined half-squares. Crib quilt has mitered borders and is quilted in a chains-of-circles pattern. Binding is folded all the way over to the backing and does not show on the front.

PATCHES: Make templates: a 1⅝" square and half-square. For each block (make 12), cut 5 squares and 16 half-squares from 1 fabric, 4 squares and 16 half-squares from contrasting fabric.

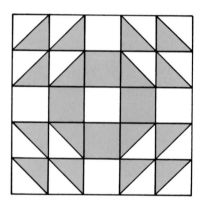

Diagram for Quilt Block

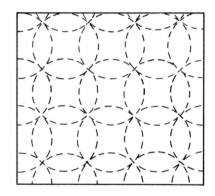

Diagram for Quilting Pattern

Wreath

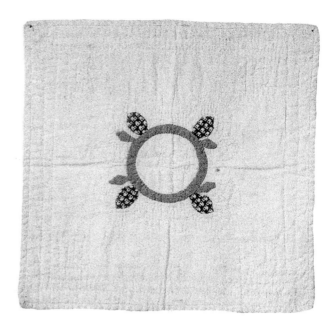

SIZE: 11¼" square

FABRICS: ⅜ yard for background, backing, and binding; scraps of 2 contrasting colors for appliqués.

NOTES: A ring with 4 buds and leaves is appliquéd in the center. Quilting follows the contours of the center design and embellishes corners and sides geometrically. Binding is of the same color, if not fabric, as quilt top and backing.

APPLIQUÉS: Make templates: trace and complete actual-size quarter pattern. Cut 1 ring, 4 buds, and 4 leaves from contrast fabrics as desired.
BACKGROUND: Cut out two 11¼" squares; do not add seam allowance. Set one aside for backing. On other, center ring; place a bud and leaf facing each corner. Sew in place.
ASSEMBLY AND QUILTING: Mark for quilting: refer to the appliqué pattern and draw double lines across center, contoured lines around wreath. Also outline quilt top with a double line, and add 2 concentric squares in each corner. Cut batting; assemble quilt layers. Quilt on marked lines.
FINISHING: Using same fabric as background and backing, make a separate ¼" binding, and attach.

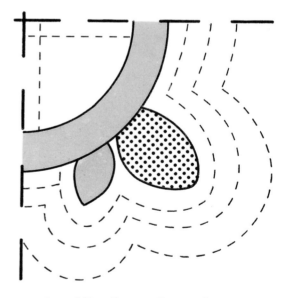

Actual-Size Quarter Pattern for
Center of Wreath Quilt

Iris. c. 1930. 38" x 60". Courtesy
of Stella Rubin Antiques

Iris

SIZE: Approximately 39¾" x 57"

FABRICS: 1⅝ yards each for backing and border; 1½ yards for hexagonal blocks to be appliquéd, ½ yard each for side blocks, leaves, and binding; ⅛ yard for stems; small amounts of assorted colors for iris petals.

NOTES: Varicolored irises are appliquéd onto hexagonal blocks and outline quilted. Antique quilt squeezes a partial appliqué design onto 2 half-blocks at center top and bottom; if desired, omit those appliqués.

Quilt has a mitered border, and is quilted in diagonal grids. Pattern is a scaled-down adaptation of a Mountain Mist Pattern. [Note: Order the patterns and instructions for making a full-size quilt, Pattern R of the Mountain Mist series (72" x 87" or 78" x 96"), from Quilt Center/Mountain Mist, 100 Williams St., Cincinnati, OH 45215, (513) 948–5307]

PATTERNS: Make templates: enlarge patterns. Make 1 full hexagonal template, 1 horizontal half-hexagon, and 1 vertical half-hexagon (A, B, and C on the diagram for quilt top). Make a separate template for each appliqué piece.

PATCHES: Cut 8 A and 2 B from the same fabric. From another fabric, cut 4 C, then cut C template crosswise in half (D) and use to cut out 4 quarter hexagons, reversing 2.

APPLIQUÉS: Use templates to cut irises as follows: cut stem from one color, leaves from a slightly different shade. Shade iris petals as desired. Position and sew an iris on each A block. Sew partial appliqué design onto 2 B blocks for center top and bottom.

QUILT TOP: Refer to diagram to arrange blocks; sew together. *BORDERS:* Add 3¾" borders, mitering corners.

ASSEMBLY AND QUILTING: Mark a 1" diagonal grid over hexagons and border, interrupting grid for appliqués. Cut backing and batting; assemble quilt layers. Quilt around irises: ¼" inside appliqués and again slightly outside them. Quilt along marked grid lines.

FINISHING: Using a contrast color, make a separate ⅜" binding, and attach.

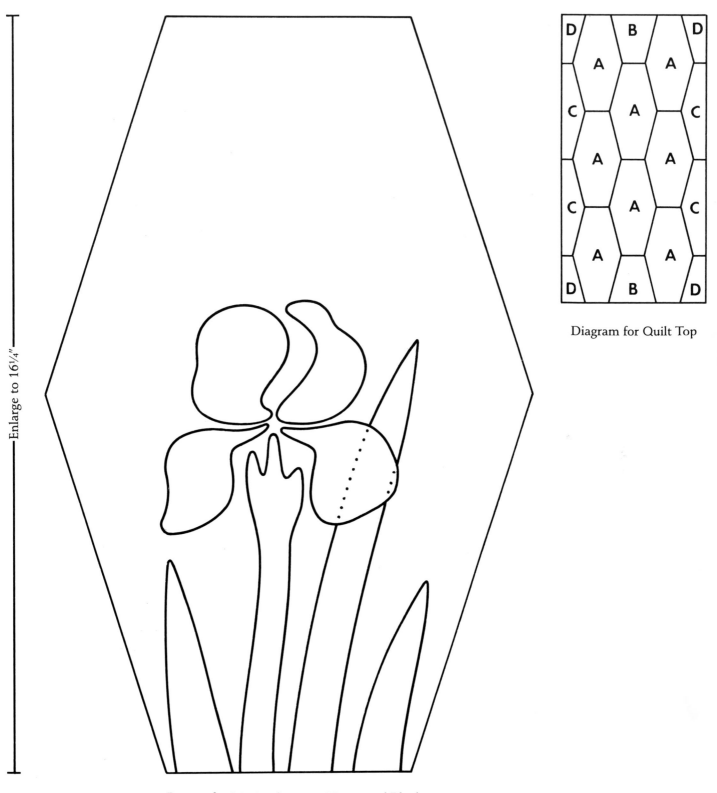

Enlarge to 16¼"

Pattern for Iris Appliqué on Hexagonal Block

D	B	D
A		A
C	A	C
A		A
C	A	C
A		A
D	B	D

Diagram for Quilt Top

Chapter 5: Multiples

Motifs that are simple or small gain strength by repetition: a little shard of glass in a kaleidoscope; the plop of a pebble in the water, rippling out in concentric circles; the chorus of a folk song. Multiplied, a motif can become more eloquent. So it is in quilts. Repetition provides rhythms that are aesthetically pleasing. Furthermore, the way these repetitions are arranged—referred to as the "set"—also affects the aesthetics.

It was well after I chose the quilts for this book that I analyzed what makes them good designs. One factor is that in each case the choice of a set is appropriate and effective for the size and scale of the quilt. It makes the difference between broken and unified, between out-of-scale and well proportioned, between monotonous and exciting.

In the Fleur-de-Lis quilt, four pretty motifs are arranged as mirror images. If the quiltmaker wanted to magnify the significance of her floral motif beyond its pretty gracefulness, she was successful. Whether she was interested in the fleur-de-lis as a Christian icon of the Trinity or the Virgin Mary, or as the element in the French emblem that represents the Flame of Light, Life, and Power, or something else, I cannot say. This small quilt was made with block-printed fabrics, probably prior to 1856. After that date, colorfast dyes were invented which quickly took the place of the block prints. The inferior dyes of the block print have left this piece vulnerable to deterioration: acids have eaten away at the printed portions, leaving a pattern of little holes all over the appliqués and border. The resulting openwork on the quilt top makes it a fascinating reminder of the fragility of all textiles.

Setting multiple blocks on their corners, or on point, often strengthens the pictorial aspect of a graphic and enables the quilter to balance her pieced blocks with plain areas that show off her quilting. This is true in both the Hourglass and Basket quilts. Made entirely by hand, Hourglass (c. 1860) is the smallest gem in this collection, only 10½" x 11½". Each block is quilted in diagonal lines and the border is quilted in zigzags. Basket offers an electric color combination: a dark navy print, which bears tan hydrangeas strewn in different directions, proves a strong contrast to the smaller-scaled yellow calico, and makes the yellow pop. Plain blocks ensure that the color play does not get too busy, yet hold their own with a bull's-eye quilting design. Sawtooth borders create a sharp, crisp frame. The backing on this quilt (c. 1880) is also noteworthy, pieced with three vertical strips of different, warm brown plaids.

A third quilt in this chapter that is set on point combines an Oak Leaf and Reel block with the Double X (or Fox and Geese) block. This crib-size piece (also c. 1880) demonstrates the attitude toward patchwork and appliqué in the nineteenth century. The Oak Leaf and Reel design, in appliqué, commands the center, and is embellished lavishly with quilted scrollwork. Patchwork Double X blocks frame the appliqué, and since it is all set on point, triangular piecework is needed to fill out the square; these are all quilted in simple, linear patterns. Assembled so unusually, Oak Leaf and Double X is a surprisingly unified design. Red and green, a color combination especially popular in the last century, help hold it together with vibrant resonance.

Displaying a straight set are two doll quilts in a Broken Dishes pattern. Undivided by framing sashes or stripping, the pattern moves continuously across each little surface. Optically schizophrenic, the design imitates little triangular shards of pottery, hourglasses, or pinwheels. The two quilts in this pattern make a striking contrast: The green and red quilt is a humble, charming representative of 1880s quiltmaking, handstitched in the popular color combination, now tinged with the patina of time. The red and white quilt (c. 1930) is entirely stitched by machine. The overlying pattern of white machine quilting in double rows on the diagonal adds durability and a clean, high-contrast spirit.

Like the Oak Leaf and Double X quilt, Framed Medallion glorifies a special center block, but it has a straight set. A Broken Star takes center stage and is bordered with several plain and pieced strips. The multiples are in the blocks that make up the pieced strips. Increasing in scale, they start out simply with sawtooth blocks, proceed in complexity to diamond-in-the-square, and climax with a swarm of Shoofly blocks. I imagine many scrapbags contributed to this rich panoply of nineteenth-century calicoes. The date (1884) of the quilt and the age (seventy-six) of the maker were included in the design. As befits its impressiveness, Elaine Hart of Quilts of America has had it nicely mounted with whipstitches over a cloth-covered, stretcher-strip frame.

The effect of multiples and their set can be seen throughout this book. Basic squares become lively checkerboards. Pandora's Box seems like six separate little quilts combined into one. Ships, Pinwheel, and Bowtie become all the more exciting visual plays. Secondary designs are created when blocks like Single Wedding Ring and Posies Round the Square combine. A single iris, when repeated, becomes a garden. In every case, the size and arrangement of the repeat motif are carefully planned for eye-catching results.

BORDERS: Using contrast fabric, add 2¼″ borders at top and bottom, 1″ borders at sides.

ASSEMBLY AND QUILTING: Refer to photograph and mark quilting lines on background. Cut backing and batting; assemble quilt layers. Quilt fleurs-de-lis ³⁄₁₆″ inside edges and on marked lines. Quilt along the center of the border.

FINISHING: Turn outer seam allowance of borders ⅛″ over twice onto backing; sew in place. Quilt all around, ⅛″ from outer edges.

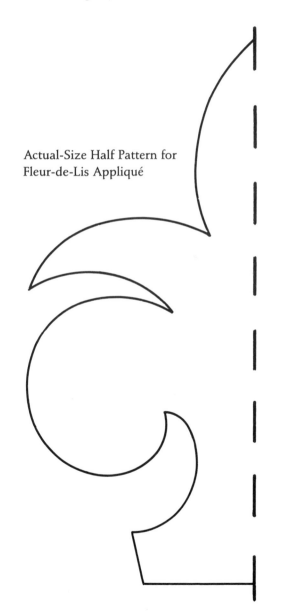

Actual-Size Half Pattern for Fleur-de-Lis Appliqué

Fleur-de-Lis

SIZE: 14″ x 16½″

FABRICS: ½ yard for quilt top and backing, ¼ yard for appliqués and border.

NOTES: In this small doll or wall quilt, 4 fleur-de-lis appliqués mirror one another. Quilt top is bordered and quilted in simple lines. Borders fold over onto the backing to bind the edges.

APPLIQUÉS: Make templates: complete the actual-size half-pattern and use to cut out 4 fleurs-de-lis from contrast fabric.

QUILT TOP: From background fabric, make a 12″ square. Fold in half horizontally and vertically; press folds to crease, open, and lay flat. Center and mark a 3″ square with a corner at each crease. Place the base of a fleur-de-lis on each side of this square; sew in place.

Basket. c. 1880. 42½″ square. Courtesy of Martha Jackson Antiques

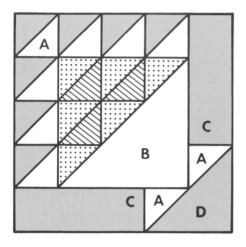

Diagram for Basket Block

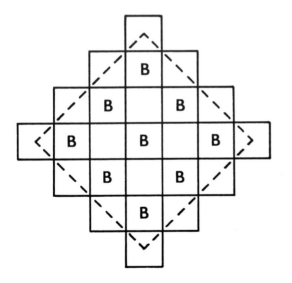

Diagram for Quilt Top
B = Basket Block

Basket

SIZE: 44" square

FABRICS: 1¼ yards for backing; 1½ yards for patches, inner and middle borders, and binding; 2 yards high-contrast fabric for plain blocks, patches, inner and outer borders; small amounts of 2 other fabrics for "contents" of baskets.
IN ADDITION, YOU WILL NEED: Quilting thread to contrast with fabrics.

NOTES: Pieced basket blocks and plain blocks are set on point and framed with pieced sawtooth and plain borders. Antique quilt is entirely hand-pieced and quilted; concentric circles embellish the plain blocks.

BASKET BLOCK (Make 9): Make templates: a 1½" half-square (A), a 4½" half-square (B), a 1½" x 4½" rectangle (C), and a 3" half-square (D). Use to cut patches for each block; refer to basket block diagram for number of patches needed from each fabric. To assemble, arrange patches as shown. Sew all A patches for basket top together in rows, sew rows together, then sew on B patch. Sew remaining A's to C's; sew to sides of basket, then sew on patch D.
QUILT TOP: Make template for a 7½" square, and use to cut out 16 plain blocks from same fabric that serves as a "background" to baskets. Refer to diagram for quilt top and arrange basket and plain blocks, with all baskets turned in the same direction. Sew together in rows, then sew rows together; set on point, as indicated by long dash lines. BORDERS: INNER BORDER: Make template for a 1⅝" half-square. Use to cut 80 from each of 2 fabrics. Sew unmatched half-squares together in pairs to form square units, then sew square units together into 4 strips of equal length. Place a strip along each edge of quilt top; butt end of each strip against side of previous strip. MIDDLE BORDER: Make 1¾" wide. OUTER BORDER: Make 2" wide. ASSEMBLY AND QUILTING: Mark quilt top as follows: On each basket block, mark from corner to corner in both directions. Within each quadrant, mark

L-shapes parallel to center lines and ¾″ apart. For whole plain blocks, mark a 2″ circle with 6 wheel spokes meeting at the center. Surround with concentric circles, each ⅝″ apart. For half plain blocks, mark concentric half-circles; for quarter plain blocks at corners, mark concentric quarter-circles. On inner border, mark a line from corner to corner on each patch, perpendicular to the diagonal seam. Over middle and outer borders, mark a scroll or chain pattern of your choosing. Cut backing and batting; assemble quilt layers. Quilt on marked lines using contrast color thread.
FINISHING: Add a separate ½″ binding.

Hourglass

SIZE: 11½″ x 12½″

FABRICS: Small amounts of 2 contrasting colors.

NOTES: Entirely hand-stitched, this miniature quilt showcases 9 pieced blocks set on point between plain blocks. The Hourglass pattern makes a pleasing aesthetic either horizontally or vertically. Considerable quilting and a thin frame of contrast binding provide the finishing.

PATCHES: Make templates: a 2″ square for plain blocks, a 1″ half-square for pieced blocks. Use to cut the following pieces: from background fabric; 16 plain blocks, and 36 half-squares; from contrast fabric, 36 half-squares.
HOURGLASS QUILT BLOCK (Make 9): Sew unmatched half-squares together in pairs to form square units. Refer to actual-size diagram and assemble 4 pairs into hourglass block.
QUILT TOP: Arrange hourglass blocks (H) and plain blocks as shown in quilt top diagram, with all H blocks turned as shown in the Hourglass Block diagram. Set on point, as indicated by dash lines. *BORDERS:* Place quilt top with all hourglasses positioned horizontally. Using background fabric, make 1¼″ borders at sides and 1¾″ borders at top and bottom.
ASSEMBLY AND QUILTING: Mark for quilting: On hourglass blocks, mark diagonal lines through center in both directions, bisecting half-squares. Mark whole plain blocks in a ⅜″ diagonal grid. Mark plain half- and quarter-blocks with concentric triangles. Mark borders in a big zigzag, filling in with concentric triangles. Cut backing and batting; assemble quilt layers. Quilt on marked lines.
FINISHING: Using contrast fabric, make a separate ¼″ binding, and attach.

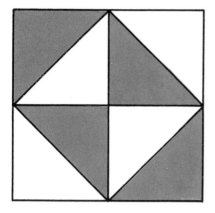

Actual-Size Diagram
for Hourglass Block

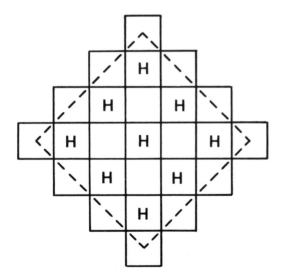

Diagram for Quilt Top
H = Hourglass Block

Hourglass. c. 1860. 10½″ x 11½″. Courtesy of Stella Rubin Antiques

Oak Leaf and Double X. c. 1880. 32″ square.
Courtesy of Stella Rubin Antiques

Oak Leaf and Double X

SIZE: 32¾" square

FABRICS: 1 yard for backing; ½ yard each of 4 different colors for background, patchwork, and appliqués, additional ⅜ yard for binding.

NOTES: Appliquéd Oak Leaf and Reel block is surrounded by patchwork Double X blocks, set on point, and filled in with triangles to complete the square. While fabrics in the antique quilt include 1 solid white, 2 red prints, 2 green prints, and 1 solid blue, fabric indications here are simplified to color 1 (background) and contrasting colors 2, 3, and 4; refer to color key. Hand-quilting embellishes appliquéd block with elaborate scrollwork, pieced sections with linear echoes of the patches.

OAK LEAF AND REEL BLOCK (Make 1): Make templates: trace and reverse pattern to make quarter pattern; rotate 4 times and cut out all oak leaves in 1 piece from color 2, reel in 1 piece from color 4. Using color 1, make background 13½" square. Center and appliqué oak leaves, then reel, on background.
DOUBLE X BLOCK (Make 4): Make templates: a 2" square (A), a 2" half-square (B), a 4" half-square (C), and a 2" x 8" rectangle (D). For each block: from color 1, cut 4 A, 10 B. From color 2, cut 4 D. From color 3, cut 4 A, 6 B, 2 C. Refer to diagram for block units to lay out and assemble the patches; for each block, make 2 of each unit. Refer to the center of the diagram for framed block to lay out and assemble these units; sew together in rows, then sew the rows together. Frame the center units as shown.
INSERT (Make 4): Cut 1 C patch from color 2, 3 C's from color 3. Piece together as shown in diagram and add a 1" strip of color 2 along the base of the joined triangle.
CORNER (Make 4): Make template for a 2¾" half-square, and use to cut 1 from color 2, 3 from color 3. Assemble as shown in diagram.

QUILT TOP: From color 1, make 8 sashing strips ¾" wide and the length of 1 side of the Double X block. Arrange blocks, sashing, inserts, and corners as shown in assembly diagram; make sure all Double X blocks are turned in the same direction. Sew together in rows, then sew rows together. Inserts and corners indicate edges of quilt; trim diagonally across outer framing corners of Double X blocks to straighten edges.
ASSEMBLY AND QUILTING: If desired, transfer a scrollwork quilting pattern of your choice to Oak Leaf and Reel block. Cut backing and batting; assemble quilt layers. Quilt center as marked or as desired. Quilt pieced blocks and sections to echo their straight lines.
FINISHING: Add a separate ½" binding.

Double X Block
Diagram of Block Units

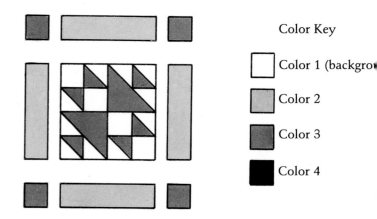

Color Key

Color 1 (backgrou

Color 2

Color 3

Color 4

Diagram of Framed Block

94

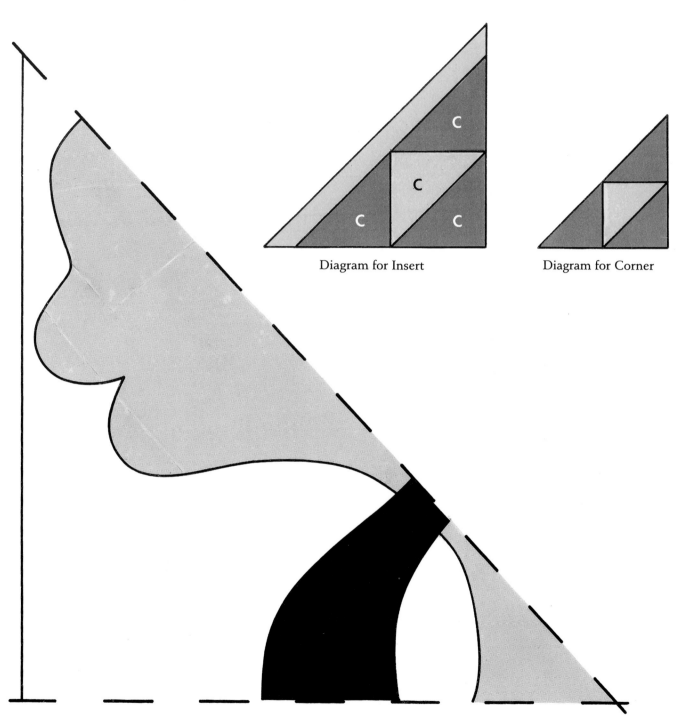

Diagram for Insert

Diagram for Corner

Oak Leaf and Reel Block
Actual Size, One-Eighth of Pattern

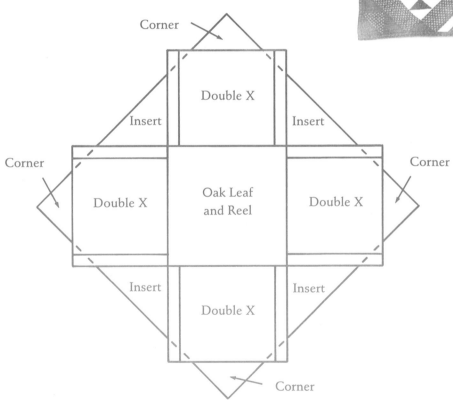

Corner

Double X

Insert   Insert

Corner   Corner

Double X   Oak Leaf   Double X
             and Reel

Insert   Insert

Double X

Corner

Diagram for Quilt Top

Left: *Hand-Stitched Broken Dishes*. c. 1880. 18″ x 19½″. Courtesy of Stella Rubin Antiques; right: *Machine-Stitched Broken Dishes*. c. 1930. 12″ x 13″. Courtesy of 'all of us americans' folk art

ℋand-Stitched Broken Dishes

SIZE: 18¾" x 21½"

FABRICS: ⅝ yard fabric for backing, patches, middle border; small amount of similar fabric for binding; ¼ yard contrast for patches, inner and outer borders.

NOTES: This doll quilt is hand-pieced, triple bordered, and hand-quilted.

PATCHES: Make template for a 2¾" half-square, and use to cut out 20 patches each from 2 contrasting fabrics.

QUILT TOP: Sew unmatched half-squares together in pairs to form square units. Refer to assembly diagram for Machine-stitched Broken Dishes quilt to arrange square units in rows, but omit right-hand square unit in each row. Alternate row 1 and row 2 for a total of 5 rows. Sew together in rows, then sew rows together.

BORDERS: Make 1⅜" inner border. Make ¾" middle border. Make 1½" outer border.

ASSEMBLY AND QUILTING: Cut backing and batting; assemble quilt layers. Quilt patches in the seams.

FINISHING: Add a separate ¼" binding.

Machine-Stitched Broken Dishes

SIZE: 12½" x 14¼"

FABRICS: ½ yard for backing, border, and patches; ¼ yard contrast for patches and binding.

NOTES: This doll quilt is machine-pieced and machine-quilted in a double line diagonal grid.

PATCHES: Make template for a 1¾" half-square and use to cut out 30 patches each from 2 contrasting fabrics.
QUILT TOP: Sew unmatched half-squares together in pairs to form square units. Refer to the diagrams to arrange and sew together in rows; alternate row 1 and row 2 for a total of 6 rows. *BORDER:* Add a 1⅝"-wide border.
ASSEMBLY AND QUILTING: Mark a diagonal 1" grid over quilt top. Cut backing and batting; assemble quilt layers. Stitch 1/16" to each side of each line.
FINISHING: Add a separate ¼" binding.

Square
Unit

Row 1

Row 2
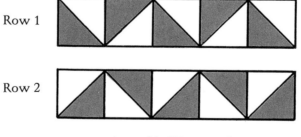

Assembly Diagrams for
Broken Dishes Quilts

Framed Medallion

SIZE: 48" square

FABRICS: 2 yards for backing, small amounts of assorted fabrics for patches and strips.

NOTES: Medallion center is a classic broken-star pattern; quiltmaker used the corner squares to embroider personal data. Medallion is framed by seven borders, both plain and pieced, which are joined around the square like the logs in log cabin patchwork. Hand-quilting embellishes center and each border.

BROKEN-STAR MEDALLION: Make templates: a 2½" square (A), a 2½" half-square (B), a diamond (C)—trace actual-size pattern. Use templates to cut the following: from light fabric, 4 A, 12 C; from medium fabric, 16 A, 8 B; from dark fabric, 16 C. Medallion diagram shows upper right quarter of broken star; arrange patches as shown. Give diagram a quarter turn clockwise to arrange lower right quarter; repeat twice more to complete arrangement. Hand-piece patches, beginning at the center and working outward.

BORDERS: Create strips for each border and attach around the center in clockwise succession like log cabin patchwork. Adjust lengths of consecutive strips as you go so that each "log" will fit across next side of quilt

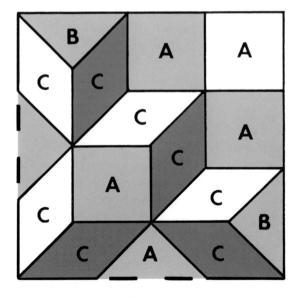

One Quarter of Broken Star Medallion

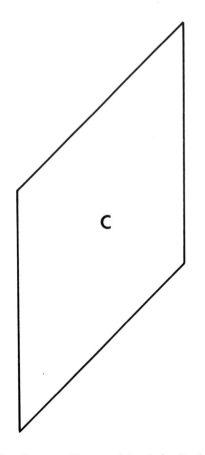

Actual-Size Pattern: Diamond Patch for Broken Star

Framed Medallion. 1884. 46½" x 44".
Courtesy of Quilts of America, Inc.

101

top. *BORDER 1:* Make a plain, 1″ border. *BORDER 2:* Make a sawtooth border: Make template for a 1½″ half-square, and use to cut 46 each from 2 different fabrics. Sew unmatched half-squares together in pairs to form square units. Sew into strips. *BORDER 3:* Make a plain, 1″ border. *BORDER 4:* Make template for a 3½″ half-square. Use to cut 24 triangles each from 2 different fabrics. Refer to the diagram and sew short sides together to form strips. *BORDER 5:* Make templates: a 2¾″ half-square (D), 2″ square (E), and 1⅜″ half-square (F). Cut 22 D's each from 2 fabrics. Join unmatched D's together in pairs to form square units. Cut 22 E's and 88 F's. Sew an F to each side of each E patch to make the square-in-square block (center block of Border 5 diagram). Alternate D units and E–F units in rows, changing the diagonal on alternate D units. *BORDER 6:*

Make a plain, 1″ border. *BORDER 7:* Make templates: a 1⅝″ square and half-square. Use to cut the following patches for each of 32 shoofly blocks: from 1 fabric, 1 square, 4 half-squares; from a contrasting fabric, 4 squares and 4 half-squares. Refer to diagram and arrange; sew together. Sew blocks together in strips. *ASSEMBLY AND QUILTING:* Cut backing and batting; assemble quilt layers. For Medallion, quilt diamonds ¼″ inside seams, and quilt squares diagonally in both directions. For plain borders, quilt in a zigzag. For Border 2, refer to short dash lines on D blocks of diagram for Border 5. Refer to short dash lines on diagrams for suggested quilting patterns for Borders 4, 5, and 7.
FINISHING: Add a separate ⅜″ binding.

Diagrams

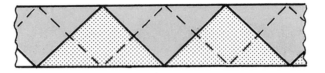

Border 4

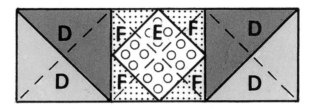

Border 5

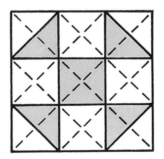

Border 7

Chapter 6: Graphics

The notion that a small quilt cannot evoke strength and power is unfounded. The graphic energy of these smaller pieces is telegraphed immediately by line, shape, and color. High color contrasts and clean, angular shapes produce strong and definitive patterns. This is not to say there are not wonderfully subtle graphics here, too. It is equally rewarding to come close and look carefully at these quilts. Then you notice the lines of the quilting patterns and the wonderful graphics of the fabrics.

In terms of energy and graphic power, no color beats red. Turkey red was the most popular color used in nineteenth-century quilts. Red fabrics were cheap, durable, and added a spot of brightness. The Amish and the Pennsylvania Deutsch obviously loved using reds throughout the early part of this century. However, the abundance of red in this book also indicates my personal predilection, and may very well have influenced my decision to include many of these quilts.

The power of the Amish Shadows pattern (called Roman Stripes outside the Amish community) is not subdued by the tiny size of this c. 1900 piece. Each square block is divided in half diagonally; only the top half is pieced, as are the border strips. In black quilting stitches on black, a heart on the black bottom half of each block is difficult to see. But such a discovery makes us appreciate the quilt even more; perhaps it served as an appropriate and loving gift for a doll-loving daughter.

The quilt pattern most representative of American nineteenth-century quiltmaking is undoubtedly the Log Cabin. Just about every quiltmaker made one. I have come across countless examples of fabulous Log Cabins. This one, made in Pennsylvania in the 1870s or 80s, was impossible to forget or exclude. The stark, high color contrast looks very contemporary. In wool, the red is almost electrified next to the black. In a Flying Geese arrangement, the blocks are archetypical of rhythmic repetition. Striped fabric in the border adds a modern touch and the cobalt blue binding surprises the viewer with its brilliant color.

As with the Log Cabin, building tools and construction techniques may have first inspired Sawtooth and Carpenter's Square designs. Their graphic power kept them popular. The crib-size Sawtooth and Cloverleaf (c. 1890) is a bonanza of cookie cutter shapes. Not only does it have four-leaf clover appliqués, but dozens of quilted stars and leaf shapes float over the surface. The doll-size Sawtooth quilt, from the 1930s and possibly Amish, looks Navajo in its arrangement of sawtooth

Amish Shadows. c. 1900. 13¼" x 16¼".
Collection of Sharon L. Eisenstat

strips. A traditional clamshell quilting design softens the angularity. Carpenter's Square (c. 1900) uses strip piecing in an elaborate construction. Its white patches are elaborately quilted with various chains of diamonds, scrolls, and ribbony scallops.

Another strip-piecing master stroke is Streak o' Lightning, from about 1880. Red and white calico half-squares are combined into strips, then staggered to form the zigzag lightning bolts. Sawtooth blocks and several plain borders frame the design.

When a single motif is graphically strong, it transcends the status of a quilt block and stands on its own as an individual quilt. Such a quilt is the Village Church. (Yvonne Khin attributes the design to *Quilt Patterns, Patchwork, and Appliqué,* from the Ladies Art Company, St. Louis, 1889; this quilt would have been made about that time.) A century ago, every church had its Sewing Society or the like. The church was a place where women found dignity, acceptance, and ethical education for their children. Perhaps this small quilt was made as a banner or emblem, or as a reminder to children of the importance of the church and of religion in their lives.

In appreciating the graphic qualities of these quilts I wonder if quiltmaking can be considered a graphic art. The larger question is whether these quilts are examples of art or craft. I think you'll agree that they are fine examples of both.

Amish Shadows

SIZE: 13⅜" x 16⅜"

FABRICS: ¼ yard dominant color for patches and inner border, ¼ yard each 4 other contrasting colors for patches, piece 15" x 18" for backing.

NOTES: Square blocks are divided into half-squares, with half cut in 1 piece from dominant color and the other half composed of 3 diagonal strips ending with a triangle. The strips are arranged in the same order to stripe the border. The solid half-square is hand-quilted with a heart. All quilting is done in black thread. The backing on this doll quilt is pieced in black and blue strips.

PATCHES: Make templates: use actual-size block pattern for patches A, B, C, D, and E. Use templates to cut 12 of each patch, using the same color for each letter throughout.

QUILT TOP: Refer to the pattern to arrange the patches for each block, and sew together. Make 12 blocks. Arrange blocks in 4 rows of 3. *BORDERS:* Using dominant color, make inner border ¾" wide. For outer border, use strip piecing: Make a ⅝"-wide strip of each remaining color across full width of fabric. Sew strips together in same order as for blocks to make a striped fabric. Cut across the stripes to make 24 strips 1¼" wide (adding seam allowance). Keeping color order consistent, sew these pieces together into 2 strips of 5 and 2 strips of 7 for borders. Attach shorter borders to top and bottom, longer borders to sides; cut off any excess.

ASSEMBLY AND QUILTING: Trace and cut out heart quilting pattern and trace onto solid half-square as shown. Cut backing and batting; assemble quilt layers. Quilt hearts and around patch A ¼" inside seams. Quilt B, C, D patches and all border strips ⅛" from long edges. Quilt E ⅛" inside all edges.

FINISHING: Add a separate ³⁄₁₆" binding.

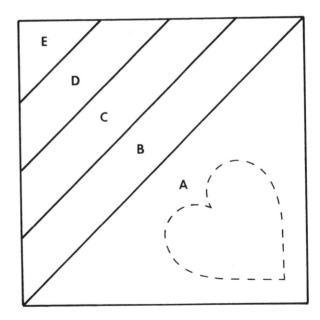

Actual-Size Pattern for Quilt Block

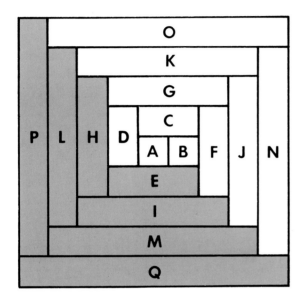

Diagram for Log Cabin Quilt Block

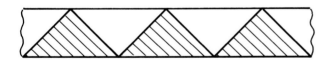

Diagram for Border

$\mathcal{L}$og Cabin

SIZE: 39⅛″ square

FABRICS: 1¼ yards muslin or similar fabric for foundation, 3 yards bright fabric for backing, logs, and border patches, 1½ yards of dark fabric for logs, small amounts of contrast fabrics for border patches and binding.

NOTES: Crib quilt is made of 36 log cabin blocks, each divided diagonally with bright patches on one half, dark patches on the other half. Logs are cut from wool fabrics and stitched to a foundation fabric; there is no batting, and no quilting within borders. Pieced border combines striped and solid fabrics.

PATCHES: Make templates: a ⅝″ square and a ⅝″-wide strip. Use strip template to cut several strips across full width of both bright and dark fabrics. Refer to diagram for quilt block: use square template to cut center A and B logs. Use strips to cut all other logs to the following lengths (add seam allowance): C and D—1¼″, E and F—1⅞″, G and H—2½″, I and J—3⅛″, K and L—3¾″, M and N—4⅜″, O and P—5″, Q—5⅝″.

Cut 36 of each patch, cutting A, B, C, F, G, J, K, N, and O from bright fabric, D, E, H, I, L, M, P, and Q from dark fabric.

QUILT BLOCK (Make 36): From foundation fabric, make 36 5⅝″ squares. Mark lines between opposite corners to divide diagonally in half in both directions. Pin center of A at intersection of lines. Refer to diagram as you sew pieces to the foundation. Place B on top of A, right sides together. Stitch along right edge. Turn B over, right side up; lightly press, and pin to hold. Place C over A and B, right sides together. Stitch along top edge, then turn C right side up, press and pin. Place D over A and left half of C, right sides together. Stitch along left edge, then turn D right side up; press and pin. Place E over A and B and bottom half of D, right sides together, and stitch along bottom edge. Turn E right side up; press and pin. First round, or concentric square, is now complete. Working in alphabetical order, sew on remaining logs in the same way.

QUILT TOP: Refer to the photograph and arrange blocks in 6 rows of 6; use the flying geese variation as shown, or experiment with other patterns. Stitching through both foundation and outer logs, sew blocks together in rows; sew rows together. *BORDER:* Make template for a 3⅜" half-square, and use to cut 36 from both bright and contrast fabrics. Refer to the border diagram and arrange 4 identical border strips: Place 8 triangles of contrast fabric with their bases all in a line. Fit 9 inverted bright triangles in between and at either end; sew together. With contrast fabric triangles on the inside, add borders to top and bottom, then sides; cut off any excess.

ASSEMBLY AND QUILTING: Place quilt top on backing. Quilt around borders along inner edge and through center.

FINISHING: Use a second contrast fabric to make a separate ¼" binding, and attach.

Carpenter's Square

SIZE: 27¾" square

FABRICS: 1 yard for backing and "background," ½ yard each of 2 contrasting colors for strips.

NOTES: A lattice design gives the impression of being appliquéd on top of a background, but it is entirely pieced of strips and small rectangles. Recreating this or a similar pattern of your own design requires that patches be marked on fabric with a T square or carpenter's square to ensure that all right angles are true. The finished quilt top is cut into a square on the bias, and double-bordered. Hand-quilting is simple on the blue patches of the actual quilt (along the seams), but elaborate on the white and red patches (scrolls, chains, ribbony scallops, diamonds, and zigzags).

PATCHES: Assembly diagram shows one half of quilt top; it would be helpful to photocopy this diagram twice and tape the 2 halves together along the long dash lines to complete the diagram.

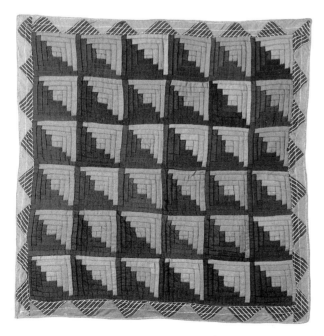

Make templates: a 1¼"-wide strip, a 3¼"-wide strip, and a 1¼" square. From each fabric, use templates to cut strips across full width, making 2 in the narrower width, and 1 in the wider width. Refer to the complete diagram and cut all required rectangular patches from appropriate strips, using the following dimensions (add seam allowance to lengths): A—3¼" square, B—1¼" x 3¼", C—1¼" x 30", D—1¼" x 25", E—1¼" x 20", F—3¼" x 9", G—1¼" x 7½", H—1¼" x 6", I—1¼" x 4½", J—1¼" x 2½", K—1¼" square (use square template).

QUILT TOP: Refer to completed quilt top diagram and arrange patches as shown. Sew patches in horizontal rows, then sew rows together, making sure that patches will "read" as continuous bars. Trim edges of quilt top to set on the bias, as indicated by short dash lines. *BORDERS:* Make a 1" inner border, 1½" outer border.

ASSEMBLY AND QUILTING: If desired, mark quilting patterns on some or all patches. Patterns for A and B patches are offered here, identical to the original quilt. Cut backing and batting; assemble quilt layers. Quilt along marked lines and/or ¼" from seams of patches. *FINISHING:* Add a separate ¼" binding.

Actual-Size Quilting Patterns

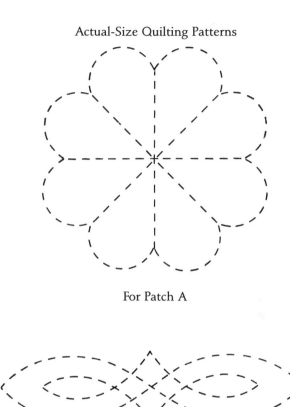

For Patch A

For B Patches

Quilt Top Diagram (Half of Quilt Top)

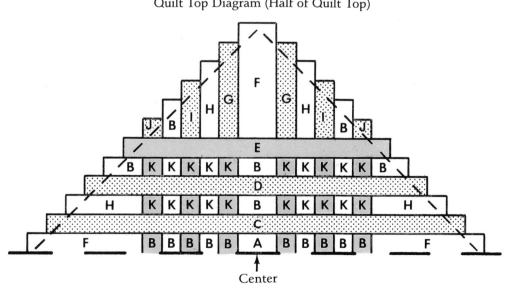

Center

Carpenter's Square. c. 1900. 27½" x 29". Courtesy of Laura Fisher/antique quilts and Americana

Sawtooth and Cloverleaf. c. 1890. 39″ square. Courtesy of 'all of us americans' folk art

Sawtooth and Cloverleaf

SIZE: 40⅜″ square

FABRICS: 3 yards for quilt top and backing, 1 yard contrast for appliqués.

NOTES: Background is cut in several sections and appliquéd, then sections are pieced. Quilting on appliqués is geometric and straight-lined. Between appliqués, quilting patterns are organic shapes. Quilt is plainly bordered, has a very thin filling, and is bound with the backing.

APPLIQUÉS: Make templates: trace and complete patterns and use to cut the following from contrast fabric: 16 A, 4 B, and 16 C.

SECTIONS: Make the following background pieces: four 13″ squares (designated Squares), eight 7¾″ half-squares (designated Small HS), and four 11″ half-squares (designated Insert).

On each Square, appliqué an A with its long straight edge centered along each edge. Appliqué a B in the center.

On each Small HS, appliqué a C in the right angle, close to seam allowances. On each Insert, appliqué 2 C's with points at center of triangle base within seam allowance and ends on opposite diagonals; see Insert on quilt top diagram.

QUILT TOP: Stitch a Small HS along its base to 2 opposite sides of each Square. Join 4 Small HS's together to form the center of quilt top. Assemble, continuing seam across corners of Squares; see quilt top diagram. Fit Inserts between squares as shown. Trim remaining corners to "square up" quilt top. *BORDERS:* Using background fabric, make 3″ border.

ASSEMBLY AND QUILTING: Mark for quilting: mark sawtooth appliqués with parallel diagonal lines ¾″ apart. Mark lines dividing cloverleafs and diamonds in half both horizontally and vertically. Mark simple leaf shapes and 5-pointed stars over background areas. Cut backing and batting; assemble quilt layers, and quilt on marked lines.

FINISHING: Bind quilt with the backing.

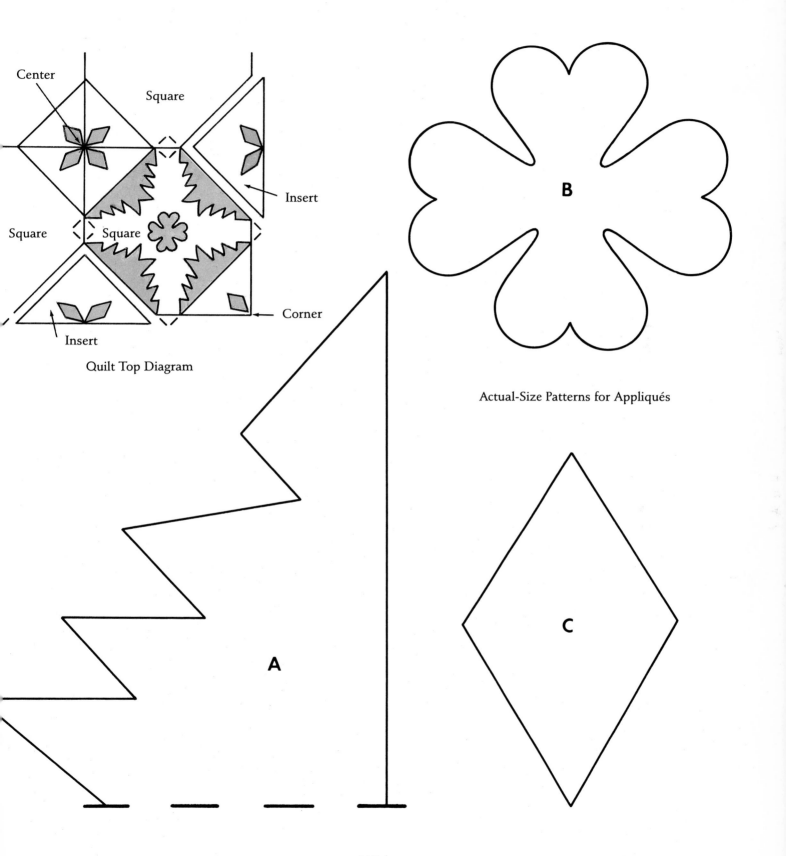

Center

Square

Insert

Square

Square

Corner

Insert

Quilt Top Diagram

B

Actual-Size Patterns for Appliqués

A

C

Sawtooth

SIZE: 31¼" square

FABRICS: 1½ yards for background color patches, backing, and binding; ⅝ yard contrast color for patches and border.

NOTES: Rows of sawtooth blocks border each segment of square-in-square-in-square patchwork. Hand-quilting combines a diagonal grid at the center with a Baptist fan or clamshell pattern around the edges.

PATCHES: Make templates: a 5" square (A); 6" half-square (B); 10½" half-square (C); 1¾" half-square (D). Refer to quilt top diagram and, from background-color fabric, cut 1 A, 4 C, and 100 D. From contrast fabric, cut 4 B and 100 D.

QUILT TOP: Sew unmatched D patches together in pairs to form square units. Refer to quilt top diagram to lay out the pieces; work from the center outward. Sew the pieces together in a logical order. *BORDER:* Using contrast fabric, make 2" border.

ASSEMBLY AND QUILTING: Mark the Baptist Fan design: set compass for a 1" radius. Place point at one corner and swing compass to scribe an arc. Keeping point of compass at the same spot, increase the radius by ⅝" and scribe another arc. Repeat until arc has a 7¾" radius. Move point of compass to where outer arc intersects edge of quilt; repeat procedure. Repeat around quilt in same manner. Mark a 1⅝" grid from center outward to meet fan pattern. Cut backing and batting, assemble quilt layers, and quilt on marked lines.

FINISHING: Using background-color fabric, make a separate ½" binding, and attach.

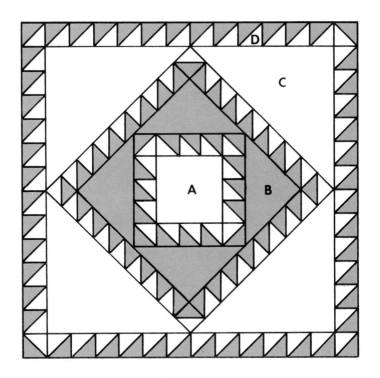

Quilt Top Diagram

Sawtooth. c. 1930. 29" square.
Collection of the author

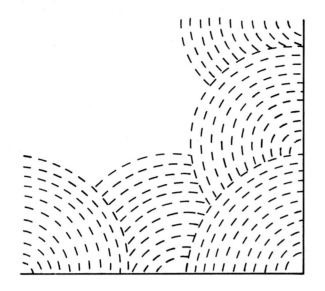

Diagram for Baptist Fan Quilting Pattern

Streak o' Lightning

SIZE: 35⅞" x 49⅝"

FABRICS: 1½ yard each of 2 different colors, for patches and borders; 1½ yards for backing.

NOTES: Half-squares are sewn together in strips; when staggered and reversed, strips make a zigzag pattern. Hand-quilting echoes the zigzag and crisscrosses the sawtooth and plain borders.

PATCHES: Make template: a 2" half-square. Use to cut 195 each from 2 fabrics.

QUILT TOP: Join unmatched half-squares along their short sides to form parallelograms, then sew parallelograms together in strips. See diagram for strip. Use 13 half-squares of each color to make 15 identical strips. Lay strips side by side. Refer to assembly diagram; turn alternate strips around 180° (Strip II) and realign, keeping 90° angles in a line across surface, creating a zigzag stripe. Sew strips together. Mark straight across at top and bottom as shown by dash lines and trim top and bottom edges, leaving seam allowance. *BORDERS: INNER SAWTOOTH BORDER:* Make templates: a 1¾" half-square and a 1¼" half-square. Use larger template to cut 64 half-squares from each fabric. Sew unmatched half-squares together in pairs to form square units. Keeping all half-squares pointing in same direction, sew units together; make 2 strips of 12 units, 2 strips of 20 units. Sew to all sides of patchwork quilt top. For corners, use smaller template to cut 8 half-squares from each fabric. Refer to diagram for border and piece. Insert at corners. *FIRST PLAIN BORDER:* Make 1" wide. *SECOND PLAIN BORDER:* Make 1" wide. *THIRD PLAIN BORDER:* Make 1¾" wide. *FOURTH PLAIN BORDER:* Make 1" wide. *FIFTH PLAIN BORDER:* Make 1" wide. *ASSEMBLY AND QUILTING:* Mark across middle of plain borders on each side of quilt. Mark diagonal lines 1" apart over plain borders, beginning from center lines and working outward, making chevrons at middle of

118

each side. Cut backing and batting; assemble quilt layers. Quilt along centers and left outline of each zigzag. Quilt around each patch of sawtooth border, just inside seams. Quilt along marked lines of plain borders.

FINISHING: Add a separate ⅛″ binding.

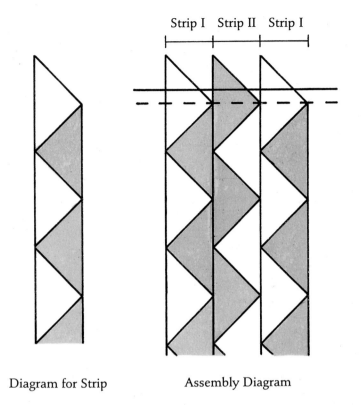

Strip I   Strip II   Strip I

Diagram for Strip   Assembly Diagram

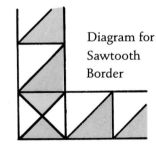

Diagram for
Sawtooth
Border

Corner

Streak o' Lightning. c. 1880. 40¼" x 52½".
Courtesy of Martha Jackson Antiques

Opposite: *Village Church.* c. 1880. 19 x 23¼". Collection
of Laurie Brzezowski and David Greenberg, courtesy of
Laura Fisher/antique quilts and Americana

Village Church

SIZE: 19⅜" x 22¾"

FABRICS: ¾ yard for background and backing; ¼ yard each of 3 contrasting colors for patchwork, appliqués, and borders.

NOTES: Patchwork and appliqué combine to build the image of a church: upper half is appliquéd to a background, lower half is pieced. Original quilt has no filling and is machine-quilted.

APPLIQUÉS: Make a 10⅝" x 7" rectangle using background fabric. Make templates: trace and enlarge pattern. Use templates to cut round window from background fabric, roof, chimneys, tower base, and spire from contrast fabric. On all pieces but window, press under seam allowance on all but lower edge. Refer to pattern and pin on background; begin with spire and work down, overlapping seam allowances. Sew in place.

PATCHWORK: Make templates from enlarged pattern; use to cut pieces for bottom half of church. Sew together walls, windows, and doorway, add upper wall, then join background rectangles, first sides, then bottom.

QUILT TOP: Sew top and bottom half of church together. *BORDERS:* Make 1" inner border, 3" outer border.

ASSEMBLY AND QUILTING: Mark a rectangle that cuts lengthwise through center of chimneys at the sides, across center of spire at the top, and along the center of upper wall along the bottom. Bisect rectangle through the center of round window. Cut backing and assemble quilt layers. Quilt around patches, appliqués, background, and inner border ½" outside edges or seams. Quilt on marked lines.

FINISHING: Add a separate ⅜" binding.

Appliqué

Patchwork

Enlarge to 14"

Pattern for Village Church

Chapter 7: Dimension

Optical illusions often provide a sense of dimension in quilt designs. Wonderful examples can be enjoyed in Laura Fisher's book *Quilts of Illusion.* Two other examples are the Square Bull's-Eye and the Contained Crazy Quilt. These quilts give me the feeling I'm peering out of a tunnel or into a mine shaft. On the 1930s Bull's-Eye, imaginary lines connecting the corners of the concentric squares take the viewer down the path of natural perspective. These illusory mitered corners lead the eye into the center. The quilt is made like a jumbo log cabin block. The crazy quilt (c. 1880) is also a variation on log cabin block construction, but with logs cut from irregular pieces and skewed. Crazy irregularities are all contained in nine little blocks, each beginning regularly with a perfect blue diamond, making it not crazy so much as endearingly eccentric.

Another optical illusion is the Basketweave design, c. 1930. Though captured in a doll-size piece, this pattern magnifies the over-and-under interplay of strands used not only in baskets but in fabrics, too. One imagines that some strands are intermittently traveling underneath others. The bright pink reads as the background, with white representing the double strands.

Finally, I present two quilts with surfaces which are actually dimensional, due to manipulations of the fabrics used. I found the Pleated Log Cabin in an antique shop, looking rather dilapidated, with some patches in shreds and the outer edges raw. It was without border or binding. I renovated it, adding the wide navy moiré binding and replacing some of the logs. In so doing, I've enhanced the design for my own enjoyment. However, as an altered piece previously in poor condition, it is not in the same league as the other quilts in the book, which are all well-preserved antiques in their original condition. This log cabin, from the 1930s or 40s, contains silks, rayons, and ribbons cut in strips. These strips are folded lengthwise in half and left unsecured along the folded edge, which is positioned toward the center of each block. The surface gives the effect of pleats, and the light-and-shadow arrangement of blocks is dazzling.

From the same period is the Yo-Yo doll quilt. The tiny scale of the rosettes, the special shape accommodating a doll's four-poster bed, and the placement of same-fabric yo-yos in vertical stripes—all add a sense of fun to the design. While purists do not categorize the yo-yo as a quilt, each individual puff, with its front and backing, can be thought of as a tiny quilt.

Quilts in this chapter do not have the monopoly on dimension. Quilting stitches provide

Bull's-Eye Square. c. 1930. 44″ square.
Collection of Mr. and Mrs. Thomas Herwitz,
courtesy of 'all of us americans' folk art

depth with subtle beauty. Because small quilts were usually hand-quilted on laps without benefit of hoop or frame, the quilting is apt to be slightly puffier. Even though traditional batting was thin and sometimes nonexistent, the quilting stitches turned two or three flat layers into one whole, three-dimensional, sculpture. The more abundant the quilting pattern, the more interesting is the dimensional interplay. Each quilted piece reads like a miniature landscape of valleys carved out by the quilting stitches. Light striking the quilt bathes the shallow hills, and shadows are cast over the valleys.

The continuing tradition of quiltmaking is taking an impressive path toward multi-dimensional manipulation. Artists like Michael James, Pamela Studstill, Nancy Crow, and Francoise Barnes, are using color for superb optical illusions that hint at at least three dimensions. Quilting stitches are being used to complement the design as never before. Unconventional techniques are being integrated with traditional ones. The small quilt is becoming a widely used format for experimentation and display.

This book looks back at the wonderful legacy of antique crib and doll quilts. I await the future of quiltmaking with equal excitement!

Bull's-Eye Square

SIZE: 45″ x 45½″

FABRICS: 1⅜ yards for backing, small amounts of assorted fabrics (4 different fabrics were used in the original).

NOTES: Quilt top is pieced much like a giant log cabin block. The quilter of the original piece was not consistent on the order in which "logs" were added, and the widths of the logs in each round do not increase in width by even increments. A recreation might be constructed more logically, by joining strips first to sides, then to top and bottom edges, and making each round ⅛″ or ¼″ wider than the previous round. (Size of the finished piece is also easily changed by making fewer or more than the 20 rounds used here.) This crib-size piece is quilted to emphasize the concentric squares; however, the last concentric round of strips folds over to the back to form a binding, then is quilted in a zigzag pattern.

CENTER: Make ½″ x 3″ strips, 3 from one color, 2 from another. Sew together along long edges, alternating colors.

STRIP PATCHES: Cut all 4 strips in each concentric square (hereafter designated a round) from the same fabric. For each round, use a fabric that contrasts with the preceeding round (although in the original, quilt rounds 14 and 15, which are made from the same fabric, break this rule). Make strips in widths as indicated below; to determine length of each strip, measure edge to be joined each time.

Round 1: ½″. Round 2: ⅜″. Round 3: ½″. Round 4: ½″. Round 5: ⅝″. Round 6: ⅝″. Round 7: ¾″. Round 8: ⅞″. Round 9: 1⅛″. Round 10: 1″. Round 11: 1¼″. Round 12: 1⅛″. Round 13: 1¼″. Round 14: 1¼″. Round 15: 1¼″. Round 16: 1⅛″. Round 17: 1″. Round 18: 1⅛″. Round 19: 2½″. Round 20: 2½″, plus ¼″ to form binding on back of quilt.

QUILT TOP: For Round 1, make two ½″-wide strips to fit sides of Center. Place one strip on top of Center, with right sides facing and left side edges even. Sew along left side. Turn strip right side up and press. Place second strip on top of Center, with right sides facing and right side edges even. Sew along right side. Turn strip right side up and press. Measure across top and bottom edges; cut two ½″-wide strips to this measurement. Place one strip on top of Center, right sides facing and top edges even. Stitch across top edge. Turn strip right side up and press. Place second strip on top of Center, right sides facing and bottom edges even. Stitch across bottom edge. Turn strip right side up and press. Round 1 is now complete. In same manner, sew on rounds 2–20.

ASSEMBLY AND QUILTING: Cut backing and batting; assemble quilt layers. Except for rounds 19 and 20, quilt all rounds 1/16″ from seams. Quilt across round 19 at approximately 2¼″ intervals.

FINISHING: Trim backing and batting smaller all around than quilt top by ¼″ plus a seam allowance's width. Fold under seam allowance of quilt top, then fold top over edge onto backing; slip-stitch in place. Quilt last round in zigzags, making angles even with quilting lines on previous round.

Basketweave

SIZE: 26½″ x 35¾″

FABRICS: 1½ yards each light and dark for patches and border, ¾ yard for backing.

NOTES: Identical blocks, alternating light and dark strips, are turned on the vertical or horizontal to create a pattern that simulates a magnification of woven fabric. Quilt is machine-pieced and machine-quilted, with outer border turned onto backing for a binding.

PATCHES: Make templates: a ¾″-wide strip and a 3¾″ square. Use strip template to cut strips ¾″ wide plus seam allowances across full width of fabrics: 11 strips from light fabric, 17 strips from dark.
QUILT BLOCK: Starting and ending with a dark strip and alternating colors, place 3 dark and 2 light strips side by side along their long edges. Sew together. Repeat with remaining strips. Use square template to trace and cut 54 quilt blocks from these pieced strips.
QUILT TOP: Place quilt blocks in 9 rows of 6. Turn each block so stripes run either horizontally (H) or vertically (V), following quilt top diagram. Sew together in rows, then sew rows together. *BORDERS:* Using light fabric, make 1″ inner border. Using dark fabric, make 1⅜″ outer border.
ASSEMBLY AND QUILTING: Cut backing and batting; assemble quilt layers. Quilt ¹⁄₁₆″ from seams on light strips and light border.
FINISHING: Trim backing and batting smaller all around than quilt top by ⅜″ plus a seam allowance's width. Turn under seam allowance on outer border and fold over edges onto backing. Slip-stitch or topstitch in place.

Quilt Top Diagram

H	V	H	H	V	H
V	H	V	V	H	V
H	V	H	H	V	H
H	V	H	H	V	H
V	H	V	V	H	V
H	V	H	H	V	H
H	V	H	H	V	H
V	H	V	V	H	V
H	V	H	H	V	H

H = Strips run horizontally
V = Strips run vertically

128

Basketweave. c. 1930. 25″ x 35″. Courtesy of Laura Fisher/antique quilts and Americana

Also make nine 4″ x 5″ rectangles from foundation fabric. For logs, cut various size and shape pieces from assorted fabrics; edges to be joined should be cut straight as you go along.

QUILT BLOCK (Make 9): Center diamond on foundation; baste in place. For round 1, begin by placing a small, roughly rectangular strip or scrap of fabric along one side of diamond, right sides together. Sew along one edge of diamond, fold scrap to right side, and press. Repeat on opposite side. Place and stitch slightly larger scraps along remaining sides of diamond. Continue adding scraps in rounds, using slightly larger pieces in each round. Diagram shows one block as an example; numbers indicate piecing order. In the actual quilt, no two blocks are the same; each incorporates different scraps and inconsistencies in the pattern. Continue to add patches until foundation is completely covered; dotted line on diagram indicates edges of foundation underneath. Trim patches even with foundation, and baste all around close to edges.

QUILT TOP: Arrange blocks in 3 rows of 3. Sew together in rows, then sew rows together.

ASSEMBLY AND QUILTING: Cut backing; assemble quilt layers. Quilt along seams of blocks.

FINISHING: Using same fabric as backing, make a separate ¼″ binding, and attach.

Contained Crazy Quilt

SIZE: 12½″ x 15½″

FABRICS: ⅜ yard for backing and binding; ¼ yard muslin for foundation; scraps of assorted colors and prints, for patches and logs.

NOTES: Doll quilt is a contained crazy patchwork, made up of 9 crazy-quilt blocks. Each block is constructed on a foundation, very much like log cabin patchwork. A diamond-shaped patch, always cut from the same fabric, is used consistently at the center of each block. "Logs" are irregular shapes, generally added in a skewed position to opposite sides of diamond. The original is hand-pieced but machine-quilted; there is no filling. Binding matches backing and is mitered at corners.

PATCHES: Make template: trace actual-size pattern for center diamond patch. Use to cut 9 from one fabric.

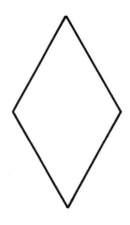

Actual-Size Pattern
for Center Diamond

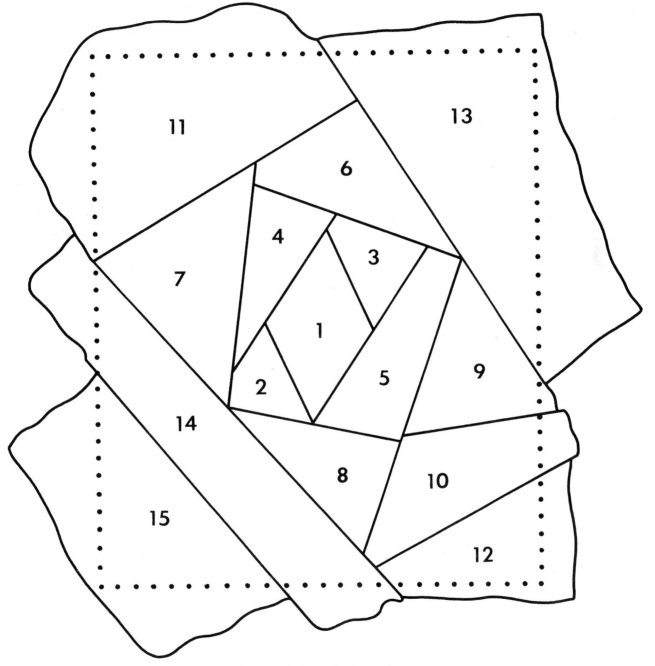

Diagram for Sample Quilt Block

Yo-Yo

SIZE: 14½″ x 17³⁄₁₆″

FABRICS: Small scraps of a variety of prints and solids as desired.

NOTES: Yo-Yos are gathered circular patches, all made from the same weight and type of fabric but different colors and prints. They are whipstitched together; the spaces left between them produce an openwork fabric. Use of same fabrics in a linear pattern produces stripes; you may plan for another pattern by grouping same color Yo-Yos as desired. Yo-Yos were left out at the bottom corners to accommodate a four-poster doll bed. As a finishing option, you may wish to back the quilt with a solid piece of fabric that will show through the openwork.
   All measurements below include ⅛″ seam allowance.

YO-YO: For each, cut out a circle of fabric just over twice the size of the desired finished Yo-Yo. Original quilt was made of 463 Yo-Yos with a finished diameter of ¹¹⁄₁₆″; for this size, start with 1⅝″ circles.
   Thread needle and knot thread ends together. Referring to Figure 1, turn under a ⅛″ hem to wrong side of circle and sew all around with small running stitches. Gather the thread up tightly and finish off by backstitching inconspicuously 2 or 3 times. See Figure 2 for finished Yo-Yo.
ASSEMBLY: Gathered side of Yo-Yo is right side. Arrange Yo-Yos wrong side up in rows to make desired quilt shape. Join with a few whipstitches where Yo-Yos touch each other; see Figure 3.

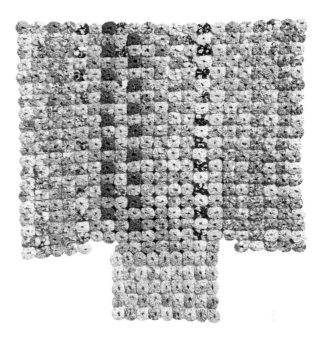

Figure 1

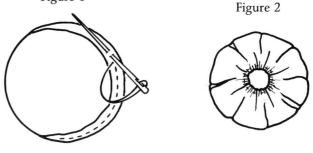

Figure 2

Figure 3

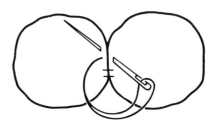

Diagrams for Stitching and Joining Yo-Yos

leated Log Cabin

SIZE: 50½" square

FABRICS: 2½ yards of 54"-wide fabric for backing and border, 2 yards muslin or similar fabric for foundation, small amounts of assorted lightweight fabrics and ribbons for "logs."

NOTES: Quilt has an arrangement of 64 log cabin blocks, each divided diagonally with bright colored patches on one half, dark colored patches on the other half. Logs are cut from rayon crepe, silk, satin, and other lightweight fancy fabrics and ribbons. They are folded lengthwise in half and stitched to a foundation fabric along the raw edges only, producing pleats across the finished block. Edges of the original quilt were unfinished; border is a recent addition.

Seam allowances are included in all dimensions given here.

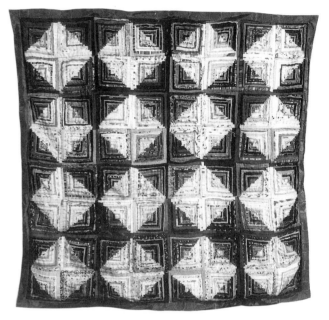

QUILT BLOCK (Make 64): From foundation fabric, cut a 7" square. Mark lines between opposite corners to divide diagonally in half in both directions. For the center patch, cut a 2" square (A). Pin center of A at intersection of lines; baste to secure.

For logs, cut 1½"-wide strips from various fabrics. Cut lengths as you go, based on the measurement of the edge you are covering; be sure to extend at least ½" beyond the diagonal creases on foundation. Refer to quilt block diagram and cut the following from light fabrics, cutting each pair from the same fabric: B and C, F and G, J and K, N and O, R and S, V and W, Z and AA, DD and EE, HH and II, LL and MM, PP and QQ. Cut the following from dark fabrics, cutting each pair from the same fabric: D and E, H and I, L and M, P and Q, T and U, X and Y, BB and CC, FF and GG, JJ and KK, NN and OO, RR and SS.

For each log, fold strip lengthwise in half with wrong side in. After you position each log, sew it in place, placing seam ⅜" from folded edge. For first round (logs B–E), cut all logs 2" in length to match side edges of A.

Beginning with B on right edge and working around clockwise, place each succeeding log over A with cut edges matching; sew each in place. For second round, place F so that it overlaps B, exposing just ¼" along the length of B, and also overlaps ends of B and C. Working in alphabetical order, continue to place and sew logs in the same way.

QUILT TOP: Refer to the photograph and arrange blocks in 8 rows of 8. Use the Light and Shadow variation as shown or experiment with another pattern. Stitching through both foundation and outer logs to expose only ¼" of outer logs, sew blocks together in rows; sew rows together.

FINISHING: Cut borders 2¼" wide and attach, mitering corners. Cut backing to same size as quilt top; assemble quilt layers. Tie or tuft quilt at intersections of blocks to secure layers. Trim backing to ½" smaller than quilt top. Turn edges of border ¼" to wrong side, fold over edges onto backing, and slip-stitch in place.

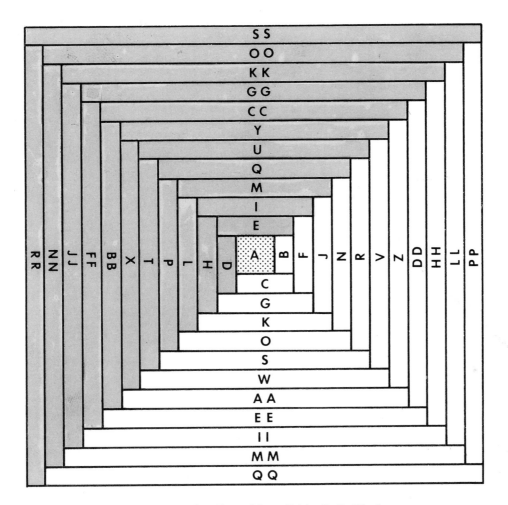

Diagram for Pleated Log Cabin Quilt Block

General Directions

There are many wonderful books available that will help the beginner learn the basics of quilting. The guidelines that follow are here to help you interpret the shorthand of this book's directions, and to suggest ways of working on a small scale. Before beginning a project inspired by one of these quilts, be sure to read through these guidelines and all the directions for the individual quilt.

SIZE: Dimensions in the directions are *not* those of the antique quilt. The captions give dimensions for each quilt; they give the largest measurement along the width and length of these irregularly shaped pieces. By contrast, the size given in the directions represents the mathematically "ideal" dimensions of a perfectly made quilt. With less than perfect templates and cutting, multiple piecing, and shrinkage from washings, there is always going to be some distortion, both in an old piece and in a new one. However, with careful piecing, your quilts should be fairly regular—i.e., rectangular—in shape.

FABRICS: The amount of fabric is suggested for making each quilt. Amount is based on cotton fabric 44" wide unless otherwise noted. Small quilts demand soft, thin fabrics even more than large quilts do, but avoid fabrics so thin that seam allowances will show through, or those that will unravel easily.

Not listed in the individual directions but necessary are the following:
MATERIALS: Sewing thread to match fabrics, quilting thread (usually white) if you will be hand-quilting, and batting. The size of the finished quilt is a good indicator of how much batting you will need; traditional, low-

loft batting or even flannel cotton fabric makes the best filler for a small quilt. Directions will note if there is no filler in the original quilt, but of course you may choose to use one in your quilt.
SUPPLIES:
Pencil
Transparent, graphed ruler, yardstick, tape measure
45° triangle for marking mitered corners
Graph paper *or* T square
Compass
Tracing paper
Dressmaker's tracing (carbon) paper and dry, ball-point pen
Water-erasable marking pen or dressmaker's marking pencil
Craft glue
Cardboard for templates
Scissors for fabric and paper
Sewing needle, #7–#10
Quilting needle
Steam iron
Straight pins
OPTIONAL:
Straight-stitch sewing machine
Cake of beeswax (to keep quilting thread from tangling)

PREPARING THE PATTERNS: Because of space limitations, some of the patterns are shown in a reduced or incomplete state.

ENLARGING: A bracket alongside the pattern indicates the length of the design in the actual quilt. Take these patterns to your local photocopy shop and ask to have the design enlarged to the specified length.

COMPLETING: Half, quarter, and one-eighth

patterns are indicated by long, heavy dash lines. Trace the pattern twice, 4 times, or 8 times, respectively, and join together, flipping alternate pieces to the reverse side and matching the dash lines. For border repeats, work from the corners inward, repeating the pattern and adjusting it so that the spacing is as even as possible.

TEMPLATES: To make these stiff patterns, trace the actual-size patterns, or draw the pattern yourself using the dimensions given. Use graph paper or a T square for marking squares and rectangles, so 90° angles will be exact. FOR HALF-SQUARES, draw a square with sides of the given dimension and cut it diagonally in half; then use the resulting triangle. TO DRAFT CIRCLES, use a compass.

Glue tracing to cardboard; let dry, then cut out. Make sure the templates are accurate so the pieces fit together properly.

SEAM ALLOWANCES: The actual-size patterns show the size of the finished patch, or the part that shows when the quilt top is assembled. **Unless otherwise noted, seam allowances are not included in any patterns or dimensions for geometric shapes, and must be added for all patchwork and appliqué.** This gives you the freedom to use the amount of seam allowance with which you are comfortable. In light of the fact that these are small quilts with proportionally smaller pieces, ¼" seam allowances are recommended. With very tiny pieces, trim seam allowance to ⅛" after sewing, to reduce bulk.

PATCHES: Lay the fabric out flat, wrong side up. Read through all directions for the project and plan for the dimensions of backing, borders, and binding before marking patches; you may want to mark patches in vertical rows to make sure you have enough fabric. However, cut out only the patches at this time. Until quilt top is assembled, you will not know exactly how long to make the borders or how large to make the backing.

Mark the patches beginning with the largest templates and proceed to the smallest. Lay the template on the fabric, placing it so as many of its straight sides are along the crosswise and lengthwise grain as possible. Using a sharp, hard pencil (light color for dark fabrics), draw around the template. Hold the pencil at an outward angle so that the point presses firmly against the template's edge. Reposition the template two seam allowance widths away and draw around it as before. Continue marking patches, but be sure not to cut the fabric until you have marked all the pieces to be cut from one fabric. When cutting, make sure you leave seam allowance. It is helpful to keep patches of the same shape and color together until you are ready to use them.

QUILT TOP: PATCHWORK: Before sewing, lay out all the pieces needed for the first block, following the directions and/or diagram. Often you will be joining several patches to create a new unit, such as a larger patch or a block. Begin by joining the smallest pieces first, then joining the larger units in rows, then joining the rows for a completed block. Take care to match seams.

To join the patches, sew by hand or machine as desired. Place 2 patches together, right sides facing and matching raw edges even. If pieces are very small, hold firmly to sew. Larger pieces can be pinned or basted, matching the points or corners first, then the marked lines in between. Pin the curved pieces together from the center out to each corner. When joining squares and rectangles, you may sew all the way across the intersecting seam allowance; otherwise, start and stop stitching at intersecting seam lines. If sewing 2 bias edges together, keep the thread taut enough to prevent fabric from stretching. As you join pieces, press the seams to one side, toward darker fabric. As you piece and press, clip into seam allowances along curves where necessary and trim seam allowance wherever there is bulk from excess fabric.

When piecing diamonds, avoid stretching by joining an edge cut along the grain to one cut along the bias. Stitch from the wide-angled corner toward the pointed end. If piecing a star design, trim seam at points as you piece.

As you work, measure each unit—blocks, rows, and so forth, to make sure it is of equal size to previous same-size units.

SETTING PATCHWORK ON POINT: Follow the

diagrams to lay out blocks into 2 "triangles" (1 inverted) which combine to form a rectangular shape with stepped edges. Use a water-erasable marker and ruler to connect the corners of the patches in continuous straight lines as indicated by the heavy, short dash lines on the quilt top diagram. This marked line is a seam line to which borders will be added; cut out beyond the marked line, leaving seam allowance.

APPLIQUÉS: The dotted lines on the patterns indicate the edge of a piece that is overlapped by another. Add seam allowance before cutting out appliqués, and press seam allowances that are not overlapped by another piece to the wrong side. Clip into curves and across points to obtain a smooth edge. Pin the appliqués to the background, overlapping pieces as indicated. Unless otherwise noted, sew each piece in place using thread in a color to match the appliqué. Slip-stitch around the edges by hand, or straight-stitch close to the edge by machine.

BORDERS: Widths, not including seam allowances, are indicated in the directions. Measure your quilt top to determine the lengths of the borders. Generally these quilts have borders attached to the shorter (top and bottom) edges first, then to those extended edges or sides.

MAKING PIECED BORDERS: Join the patches as indicated, then adjust and center the border so that the design works as neatly as possible at the corners.

MITERING BORDER CORNERS: Sew extra long border strips to all sides of the quilt top, with an equal amount extending at each end; do not stitch beyond the corners of the quilt top. Lay the quilt top flat, right side down. At each corner, hold adjacent ends of the border strips together with right sides facing. Keeping the quilt flat, pin across the borders diagonally from the quilt top corner at a 45° angle; baste, then stitch on the basting line. Cut excess fabric beyond seam; press seam open.

ASSEMBLY AND QUILTING: Prepare for quilting: Mark any necessary quilting lines on quilt top before layers are assembled. For simple, straight-line designs, experienced quilters work without markings and follow the seam or visualize the diagonal lines that connect corners. They may also apply strips of masking tape to the assembled quilt for straight lines to guide their stitching. However, you may prefer to mark lines before assembling the layers, using a water-erasable marking pen and a ruler. For more complex designs, transfer the design using dressmaker's carbon. Quilting patterns are indicated with short, fine dash lines.

BACKING AND BATTING: Unless otherwise indicated, cut the backing and batting 1" larger all around than the quilt top.

ASSEMBLING QUILT LAYERS: Place the backing, wrong side up, on a flat surface. Place the batting on top and smooth it out. Baste by tacking huge stitches in a cross. Place the quilt top on the batting, right side up. Pin, then baste through all thicknesses, using a contrasting color thread on a large needle. Start at the center of the quilt, baste outward in all directions, then baste all around the edges of the quilt top.

QUILTING: For small quilts, a frame or hoop is not necessary. Begin in the center of the quilt and stitch toward you, turning the quilt every so often in order to work outward in all directions evenly. To hand-quilt, use quilting thread and strive for even running stitches. To machine-quilt, use sewing thread and set the machine for 6–8 stitches per inch.

FINISHING: ADDING A SEPARATE BINDING: Trim the backing and batting even with the quilt top. Cut strips twice the width of the finished binding (as noted in the directions) plus seam allowance. Most of the quilts in this book have the binding cut along the grain, though you may prefer to cut it on the bias, for easing around corners. Piece strips together until they are more than long enough to go around the quilt. Press the seam allowance to the wrong side on one long edge. Pin the other long edge to the quilt top; miter or ease at the corners. Stitch all around, through all layers, leaving the appropriate seam allowance; trim and finish the ends neatly. Pin the pressed edge to the seam line on the backing; slip-stitch in place.

BINDING WITH THE BACKING: Trim the batting even with the quilt top; cut the backing to extend ½" beyond. Press the excess in half and fold it over onto the quilt top; pin the top and bottom first, then sides. Slip-stitch or top-stitch to secure.

Acknowledgments

I would like to express my thanks to the following people, without whose friendship and talents this book would not have been possible:

To Hiroko Otani Kiiffner, an eminently sensible, professional lady. I am so lucky to have her as my literary agent.

To all those gracious dealers and private collectors who consented to let me use their fine quilts in this book. Mentioned by name in the captions and Dealers listing at the back of this book, each has my utmost appreciation.

To André Gillardin, the fastest and the finest photographer. His involvement, expertise, sensitivity to the subject matter, and good nature made the shooting days very enjoyable. Michael Phillips' competent assistance enabled us to accomplish the tasks at hand with incredible speed.

To Robin Tarnoff, a superlative graphic designer who bestowed her creative flair on the design for this book's prototype.

To Roberta Weiss Frauwirth, whose meticulous illustrations are the best in the business.

To Ellen Rosefsky and Lois Brown, my editors, and Darilyn Lowe, the book designer, for their thoughtfulness and enthusiasm, and to my friend Carol Spier, who gave a sharp editorial eye to shaping and correcting the directions. It is their efforts that save me from cringing humility.

For the help and inspiration provided by Connie Matricardi, Susan Frushtick, and Sharon L. Eisenstat, who collaborated with me on the photo-styling.

To the colleagues and friends who opened up their lovely homes or workplaces for photography: Martha Jackson of Martha Jackson Antiques, Elaine Hart of Quilts of America, New York City, Judith Milne of the Judith and James Milne Gallery, New York City, Connie and Rob

Walkingshaw, Patricia Long Gardner, Sandy and Patrick Dolan, Tracy and Dave Tolme.

      To the Goodwives Quilters of the Darien Historical Society for their criticism and support, and for giving me a firsthand understanding and appreciation of quilters' groups. Thanks, also, to the Central Oklahoma Quilters Guild, Inc., for their research assistance in pattern sources.

      To Nancy Campbell, Director of Collections at Kraft/General Foods, for generously sharing her resources with me.

      To Marc Silver, Penny Kaganoff, and Carol Sterbenz who unselfishly welcomed me onto their footholds in book publishing, and Betsy Emery, my mentor in quilt instructioning.

      Thanks to Marsha Dale, Maya Dale Silver, and Jane Matricardi for helping to get such adorable poses out of baby model Daniella Dale Silver.

      Thanks for the contributions of props and both material and emotional support from: Ruth Levie and Eleanor Harrington, Mary Hillery, Carol Ciuffo, Sammie Moshenberg, Hulda Waterston, Barbara and James Emmett, Betsey Neale, Joan Dillon, Sweet Nellie in New York City, and the Thomlinson Gallery in Baltimore, Maryland, which lent me the whimsical wrought-iron bird by Bill Heise and beautiful white porcelain vase by George Zarolinski.

      Most special thanks to my wonderful husband and best critic, Carl Harrington, who gave me the freedom and active support that saw me through every aspect of this project.

The Donkey and Elephant designs are used with permission of The Kansas City Star Co., Kansas City, MO. The Iris design is used with permission of the Mountain Mist Pattern Collection of Stearns Technical Textiles, Inc., 100 Williams St., Cincinnati, OH. The Sunbonnet Ladies quilt is in the collection of The Darien Historical Society, 45 Old King's Highway, North Darien, CT, 06820.

Dealers

Many of the quilts shown in this book were available for viewing and/or purchase at the time of writing this book. For further information on these and other antique quilts, contact the following sources.

'all of us americans' folk art. Bettie Mintz, P.O. Box 5943, Bethesda, MD 20014. (301) 652–4626

Laura Fisher/antique quilts & Americana. 1050 Second Ave., Gallery 57, New York, NY 10022. (212) 838–2596

Martha Jackson Antiques, Main Street Cellar. 120 Main St., New Canaan, CT 06840. (203) 966–8348 or (203) 637–2152

Judith and James Milne, Inc. American Country Antiques, 506 East 74th St., New York, NY 10021. (212) 472–0107

Susan Parrish Antiques. 390 Bleecker St., New York, NY 10014. (212) 645–5020

Quilts of America, Inc. 431 East 73rd St., New York, NY 10021. (212) 535–1600

Stella Rubin Antiques. 12300 Glen Road, Potomac, MD 20854 (301) 948–4187

Cathy Smith antique quilts. P.O. Box 681, Severna Park, MD 21146. (301) 647–3503

Yankee Doodle Dandy. 1974 Union St., San Francisco, CA 94123. (415) 346–0346

Bibliography

Cooper, Patricia and Buferd, Norma Bradley. *The Quilters, Women and Domestic Art.* New York: Doubleday & Co., Inc., 1977.

Ferrero, Pat, Elaine Hedges, and Julie Silber. *Hearts and Hands, The Influence of Women & Quilts on American Society.* San Francisco: The Quilt Digest Press, 1987.

Fisher, Laura. *Quilts of Illusion.* New Jersey: Main Street Press, 1988.

Fox, Sandi. *Small Endearments: 19th-Century Quilts for Children.* New York: Charles Scribner's Sons, 1985.

Gutcheon, Beth. *The Perfect Patchwork Primer.* New York: Penguin Books, 1973.

Hall, Carrie A. and Rose G. Kretsinger. *The Romance of the Patchwork Quilt in America.* Idaho: Caxton Printers Ltd., 1935 with recent editions published by Bonanza Books, a division of New York: Crown Publishers, Inc.

Johnson, Bruce. *A Child's Comfort, Baby and Doll Quilts in American Folk Art.* New York: Harcourt Brace Jovanovich, with the Museum of American Folk Art, 1977.

Khin, Yvonne M. *The Collector's Dictionary of Quilt Names and Patterns.* Washington, D.C.: Acropolis, 1980.

Martin, Nancy J. *Pieces of the Past.* Bothell, Washington: That Patchwork Place, Inc., Second Edition, 1986.

Newman, Molly and Barbara Damashek. *Quilters* (musical). New York: Dramatist's Play Service, Inc., 1986.

Orlofsky, Patsy. "The Collector's Guide for the Care of Quilts in the Home." *The Quilt Digest 2,* San Francisco: The Quilt Digest Press, 1984.

Pellman, Rachel and Kenneth Pellman. *Amish Crib Quilts.* Pennsylvania: Good Books, 1985.

————. *The World of Amish Quilts.* Pennsylvania: Good Books, 1984.

Schaefer, Becky. *Working in Miniature, A Machine Piecing Approach to Miniature Quilts.* California: C & T Publishing, 1987.

Woodard, Thomas K. and Blanche Greenstein. *Crib Quilts and Other Small Wonders.* New York: E. P. Dutton, 1981.

————. *Twentieth Century Quilts, 1900–1950.* New York: E. P. Dutton, 1988.